EDUCATING CHILDREN AT HOME

Also available from Cassell:

C. Erricker, J. Erricker, D. Sullivan, C. Ota and M. Fletcher: *The Education of the Whole Child*
S. Wolfendale: *Empowering Parents and Teachers*
S. Wolfendale and K. Topping: *Family Involvement in Literacy*

Educating Children at Home

Alan Thomas

CASSELL

Cassell
Wellington House
125 Strand
London WC2R 0BB

370 Lexington Avenue
New York
NY 10017–6550

First published 1998

British Library Cataloging-in-Publication Data
A catalogue record for this book is available from the British Library.

ISBN 0–304–70179–3 (hardback)
    0–304–70180–7 (paperback)

Typeset by York House Typographic Ltd, London
Printed and bound in Great Britain by
Redwood Books, Trowbridge, Wilts

Contents

To my family

Preface

First and foremost I want to thank the one hundred families, in Australia and Britain, for welcoming me into their homes and for sharing their experience of home education with me.

I am particularly indebted to the co-ordinators of home education networks in Australia and Britain: Leslie Barson, Kathleen Carins, Georgie Holderness-Roddam and Jane Lowe. They facilitated initial contact with families, gave me help and advice in many ways and commented on various sections and drafts of the book. I would also like to thank Paula Bell and Dr Amanda Petrie for their comments on the manuscript.

The study was supported by generous research leave while I was at the Northern Territory University in Darwin, Australia. Part of the British research was carried out while I was a Visiting Fellow at the University of London Institute of Education.

I would like to acknowledge the help given by members of the following organizations:

Education Otherwise (UK)
Home Education Advisory Service (UK)
Home Educators Networking, Tasmania
The Otherwise Club (London)
Tasmanian Home Education Advisory Council

Finally, I would like to thank my former psychology and education students at the Northern Territory University for their helpful and insightful comments on the research as it progressed.

NOTES

Home education is often referred to as home schooling or, in the UK, as 'education otherwise' or 'EO'.

Each of the families is identified by case number. Australian families are numbered 1–58; British families, 59–100.

Chapter 1

Introduction

A small but increasing number of parents/carers opt to educate their children at home. The main purpose of this book is to describe how they set about it. Their experiences, as they come to grips with the task, yield new and often fascinating insights into the nature of intellectual development and learning.

Children are born, they learn to walk, they learn to talk, they go to school. Schooling is now so ingrained in our culture we have come to believe there can be no education without it. In line with this, almost everything done to improve the quality of education, through research and innovation, is based on the assumption that schooling and education are interchangeable terms. This is understandable because children have almost without exception gone to school, at least since the middle of the nineteenth century. But the consequence has been to prevent us from thinking about other ways of educating children. The belief has grown that what applies to teaching and learning in school must have universal application.

Although there are many and varied methods of teaching and learning in the classroom, often the subject of heated debate, there are certain fundamental expectations governing education in school. It is assumed that in order to be educated effectively, children need to start school at an early age, by 5 at the latest. They need to be taught within a structured framework for five or so hours a day for about twelve years. Four-year trained graduate teachers, backed by a professional body of knowledge, resources, supervision, guidelines and school policy, plan in detail how the children in their class will learn. They are supported by a carefully researched, graded curriculum, determined at national or local level and regarded as a prerequisite for good teaching and essential for effective learning. Children are expected to progress step by step through pre-ordained sequences and to provide evidence of learning, mostly through written work.

With all this in mind it is understandable that parents, when they embark on home education, should attempt to put into practice what might be loosely termed this school model, with timetables and carefully prepared lessons, only to discover that what works in the classroom does not transfer easily into the home. Of necessity they become pioneers of a different pedagogy, more suited to learning at home. Their experiences, as they adapt, yield very different perspectives on education and challenge many professional assumptions about the nature of teaching and learning.

It is only during the last two decades or so that home education has gradually come to be more widely accepted as an alternative to school. During this time, the number of children being educated at home has grown steadily, especially in Western Europe, North America and Australasia, though there are no reliable prevalence estimates. This is partly because, in many countries or states, parents whose children have never been to school are not required to register with any authority. Another reason is that many education authorities or departments lose track of children withdrawn from school. The highest prevalence is almost certainly in the United States where about half a million (1 per cent) children probably have experience of home education (Lines, 1991). In the UK it is estimated that up to 10,000 families educate their children at home (Meighan, 1997; Petrie, 1998). Between 10,000 and 15,000 children in Australia are believed to be educated at home (Hunter, 1995). But these are only estimates. As Lines (1995) points out, accurate estimates of prevalence will not be available until a well-designed household study is carried out.

The research described in this book was undertaken in Australia and England. In Australia there are eight States and Territories, each with its own laws covering home education (Hunter, 1995). In general, home education is permitted or at least tolerated. In the State of Tasmania, where nearly all the Australian research was undertaken, home educators used to keep a very low profile and few registered. Recently, however, the Tasmanian State Government, acknowledging the reality of increasing numbers of home educators, officially recognized home education for the first time in a new Education Act. Guidelines for intending home educators have been published and it is now a legal requirement for each child to be registered and monitored (Carins, 1995; THEAC, 1996). An advisory council has been set up, chaired by a home educator. The first government official appointed to register and monitor home educating families was also a home educator.

Home education has always been legal in England and Wales; the 1944 Education Act states education is compulsory, 'either by regular attendance at school or otherwise'. The 1996 Education Act contains the same provision. Various networks and organizations publish guides for intending home educators (e.g. Education Otherwise, 1993; Home Education Advisory Service, 1996). Local education authorities have the duty of fulfilling the national requirement of ensuring children receive an education in accord with their individual needs, which they exercise in varying ways and to varying degrees. In the past, authorities were often obstructive and legal wrangles sometimes ensued, but the last two decades have seen a gradual change towards tolerance and even support in some instances (Petrie, 1998).

In most other countries or states in Australasia, North America and Europe, with a few exceptions, nearly everyone who wants to home educate is able to, although there is sometimes conflict with the authorities. The New Zealand government actually provides financial assistance for home educating families.

Home education has attracted little research interest. This is surprising when one considers that it provides a unique opportunity to study teaching and learning other than in school. What research there is tends to treat it as a social phenomenon, dealing mainly with its historical development, what leads parents to educate their children at home, legal and political issues, and dealings with educational authorities and professionals (Mayberry *et al.*, 1995; Meighan, 1984a, 1984b; Paterson, 1995; Petrie, 1992, 1993, 1995; Van Galen and Pitman, 1991; Webb, 1990). Although academic outcomes have been shown to be favourable (Lines, 1995; Meighan, 1995, 1997; Ray, 1997; Ray and Wartes, 1991) there has never been a systematic attempt to find out how parents actually go about teaching their children at home, the main focus of this book.

THE RATIONALE BEHIND THE RESEARCH

My research into home education was prompted by two related theoretical perspectives, described in detail in the next two chapters. The first arises from educational research and the second from research in developmental psychology.

The first arose from my interest in individualized teaching (Thomas, 1992). There is a philosophical conviction which goes back more than two thousand years, that the meeting of two minds is fundamental to the pedagogical process. Endorsed by Rousseau, John Dewey, the Child Study Movement and the Plowden Report, this philosophy dominated educational thinking and the training of teachers until relatively recently. Although many teachers subscribed to the philosophy, it was not until the 1980s that the manifest impossibility of teaching children individually in the classroom was finally documented (Bennett *et al.*, 1984; Galton, Simon and Croll, 1980).

Even though children cannot be taught individually in school, the belief that somehow they should be will not go away. The rhetoric of school policy statements still routinely refers to catering for the individual child. Academics fuel the rhetoric in teacher training textbooks. Here is just one out of a myriad of examples:

> Each learner has unique characteristics and learning problems. One of the teacher's main tasks is to identify those characteristics and problems (diagnosis) and create appropriate learning conditions (treatments) which will enable that individual to reach required levels of competence. (Child, 1985, p. 22)

This fruitless preoccupation with trying to individualize teaching in the classroom would be unnecessary if other teaching methods were satisfactory. There has been an immense effort to improve classroom teaching and hence academic achievement, accompanied by an awesome amount of research, all of which has made little apparent difference to the quality of education. Time-honoured methods, based on good discipline combined with keeping noses to the grindstone or, in current parlance, good classroom management coupled with maximizing 'on task' behaviour or Active Learning Time, have not been superseded. A number of researchers, albeit reluctantly, conclude that such methods may represent optimal classroom pedagogy and that no substantial improvement is likely ... until teachers are somehow enabled to interact with individual children (Bennett and Desforges, 1985; Wells, 1986). But not one professional or academic educator is able to suggest how this is to be achieved.

In fact, in spite of nearly a century of interest in individualized teaching, practically nothing is actually known about it in practice, certainly not with regard to children of school age, simply because it cannot be studied to any significant extent in school. The only way to find out more is to turn to children who are educated at home.

The second perspective concerns more informal and incidental aspects of individualized teaching and learning which occur largely through social conversation with an adult (Thomas, 1994). I was introduced to this aspect of learning during my first encounter with a home educating family with whom I was invited to spend a week 'living in'.

What impressed me most during that week was that nothing much seemed to happen, on the surface at least, especially when compared with the sense of purposeful industry you get when you look into a typical classroom. There was no timetable or sequentially designed programme of learning activities within a planned curriculum. We went for walks. The two children, aged 11 and 13, certainly read a lot. They spent some time working on their own projects. There were various outside activities, including band practice. One of them was doing a project on infant development and was helping a neighbour with her newborn baby. There were friends around after school and there was a schools' musical Eisteddfod which one of them took part in. They certainly did not apply themselves to learning in the way children in school do.

Yet these children certainly were learning, though obviously not through the kind of organized individualized teaching I had expected to see. What struck me most of all during the week was the constant opportunity for informal learning, especially through social, often incidental conversation. Whether they were out walking, sitting around the kitchen table, engaged in some other activity such as drawing, making something, working on a project, eating, out in the car, or even reading, there was an incredible amount of spontaneous incidental talk. One day, for example, we were all sitting around the kitchen table engaged in our separate activities. Topics of conversation, as often as not unrelated to what we were doing, kept cropping up. Among other things, we discussed slavery, Nelson Mandela, salt-water crocodiles and levels of groundwater … and whether to go down to the shop for some doughnuts. The children probably saw this as no more than social chat. But I wondered how far this kind of incidental learning might contribute to their overall education. With or without it, they were certainly making progress. Both have since gone on to study part-time at adult and further education classes and to successfully take public examinations.

In school, children rarely have the opportunity for such potentially enriching social conversation with adults. It is strongly reminiscent of the way nearly all children learn before they go to school, exemplified in the celebrated research into early learning of 3- to 4-year-old children undertaken by Tizard and Hughes (1984), even though the children I stayed with were 11 and 13 years old.

During the first few years of life all children learn a tremendous amount without being deliberately taught, much of it through social, informal, everyday conversation. We do not deliberately or consciously teach children language but they still learn its highly complex structure. Children can informally acquire two or even three languages at the same time. Similarly, most children pick up fundamental number and literacy skills before they go to school. They learn to count, the conceptual basis for addition and subtraction, letter recognition and other literacy basics. They also acquire a tremendous amount of general knowledge. It is surprising just how much we expect children to know by the time they do arrive at school. And nearly all this learning happens informally, in a welter of chaotic haphazardry. Yet, somehow or other, all the bits and pieces manage to coalesce into a coherent body of knowledge about the culture in which the child has been reared.

A further stimulus for the research derives from the study of early (preschool) intellectual development of gifted and talented children. Bloom (1985) and Howe (1990) demonstrate the part played by both individualized teaching and informal, conversational learning in markedly accelerated intellectual development and gifted-ness. It is not giftedness itself which is of interest here. Very few home educating parents are interested in 'hothousing' their children or trying to create prodigies, although it is true that a few home educated children make startling progress. What is of interest is the potency of the pedagogy and its potential contribution to intellectual development *after* children reach school age.

THE SCOPE OF THE BOOK

The theoretical background, briefly summarized above, is explained in detail in Chapters 2 and 3. Chapter 4 provides a backdrop to the research, describing why the parents in the study decided to educate their children at home. The bulk of the research, from Chapters 5 to 9, deals with how they go about the task.

Although parents vary greatly in the way they educate their children, even different children in the same family, they virtually all share one thing in common which is that their approach becomes less formal with time. The terms 'formal' or 'informal' are not used in the way they are commonly used in school, to differentiate between classroom teaching methods. I use 'formal' only to refer to the fact that teaching in school is formally organized, with a prescribed curriculum, carefully sequenced and graded, taught within a structured framework and with an emphasis on written work as evidence of learning. It is what most people, including most professional (and home) educators, expect home education to be like when they first encounter it. They have no other model.

Even a more formal, structured approach to teaching and learning at home, described in Chapter 5, turns out to be rather different from school. The principal difference is that, because it is one-to-one, with the parent more or less constantly at hand, any question arising or problem encountered is dealt with there and then, at length if necessary. In consequence, learning becomes a continuous process with very few errors and attendant feelings of failure.

Chapter 6 describes how most parents gradually modify their initially more formal approaches, partly influenced by their children's resistance to 'lessons', school-type exercises and direct teaching. A few parents find they do not need to modify greatly a more formal, structured approach. A few abandon formal teaching and learning altogether. The majority, understandably given the untested nature of informal learn-ing, strike a balance.

Chapter 7 focuses on informal learning and shows how it can be conceived of as an extension of learning in early childhood, intellectual progress occurring by osmosis, rather than as a result of deliberate teaching, through day-to-day living experiences. The role of the parent is just as crucial as it is in more formal teaching and learning, if not more so, because there is no set curriculum to fall back on.

Chapter 8 is entirely devoted to just one aspect of one child's informal learning, taken from her mother's very detailed journal of home education. It demonstrates, at a micro level, how informal learning actually does lead to visible increments in learning, even in a subject as formally structured as maths.

Much more space in the book is devoted to informal learning. This is because it borders on the far-fetched to suggest that children can progress at the same rate as children in school, simply from what they absorb through everyday living. Such a proposal obviously requires detailed treatment.

When I embarked on this research I did not expect to be giving much attention to literacy, dealt with in Chapter 9. As might be expected, parents use a variety of methods to teach reading as they tailor their approach to each child. Of greater interest, and a good measure of the parents' success in teaching reading, is that home educated children generally become enthusiastic, often insatiable readers. Most surprising, and intriguing, is that a significant number of children do not learn to read until very late, between 8 and 10 years of age, apparently without detriment.

Chapter 10 deals with the major criticism home educators face from relatives, friends and acquaintances, which, curiously, does not concern academic progress or the ability of untrained parents to educate their children at home. Rather it is that children will be deprived of social contact with peers and lack experience of the real world outside the home. It goes without saying that home educated children have limited opportunities for mixing with other children of the same age. Parents are acutely aware of this and go to great lengths to compensate. However, as they see their children grow up, apparently normal, and at ease socially, they begin to challenge the general view that school is necessary for healthy social development. Some go further and suggest it is school which is not in the real world and that the institutional nature of schooling, along with its restrictive peer culture, may actually impede and even distort healthy social development.

Chapter 11 draws together what the study of children being educated at home can contribute to our understanding of the nature of teaching and learning.

THE FAMILIES

As explained above, there are no reliable registers of home educated children kept by education authorities or any other organization. Therefore, obtaining a representative group of families is out of the question. The difficulty is the greater because many home educators are apprehensive of outsiders. They generally have direct experience of, or at least have heard about, unpleasant confrontations with education and child welfare professionals. There is also a wariness of professionals or researchers who are perceived as inspectors, especially so by parents who have no post-school qualifications (see Van Galen and Pitman, 1991; Webb, 1990).

Nearly all the participating families were contacted through co-ordinators of non-aligned, loose networks of home educators in Australia (Tasmania) and England (London and Home Counties). In some cases, participants themselves suggested other home educators and contacted them to pave the way for an approach. Religious or other ideologically committed organizations of home educators were not approached, though a few members of such groups were included because they had also joined a non-aligned network. Hence the participating families are characteristic of those who have their own particular reasons for home educating, with few motivated primarily by ideological, mainly religious commitment.

Home educated children are not available to researchers in serried ranks according to age and organized into convenient groups of 30 or so. The extremely diverse nature of the participants in this study requires some comment. They consisted of families with a child or children of school age who were being, or had very recently been home educated. Parents had been home educating for anything between a few months and twenty or so years. Parents also ranged from those who had decided to home educate before their children were born to those who would never have entertained the idea until they came to believe that problems in school had reached such a pitch as to leave them no alternative. Some children had been in and out of school. Some home educated children had siblings in school. The ages of the children ranged from 5 to 17.

Table 1.1 provides a breakdown of basic information about the 100 participating families. The purpose is to provide background information for this group only. Two further families withdrew after initially agreeing to take part, one before and one after interview.

Table 1.1 *Family characteristics*

	Australia	England	Total
Number of families	58	42	100
Responsible parent(s)			
Female	47	36	83
Both	11	4	15
Male	0	2	2
Single-parent families (all female)	9	5	14
Level of education			
At least one parent a teacher	16	13	29
Other graduate	12	11	23
No post-school qualification	30	18	48
Number of children being home educated			
One in family	22	22	44
Two	16	14	30
Three	7	4	11
Four	10	1	11
Five+	4	0	4
Families with other children currently in school	17	9	26
Age and sex of children	*male*	*female*	
≤ 7	35	30	65
8–10	43	28	71
11–13	25	22	47
14+	15	12	27
Total children	118	92	210

It is plain that home education, in these families at least, is predominantly a female occupation (cf. Paterson, 1995). Few share the task and only two males have primary responsibility for it. In between a quarter and a third of the families, one of the parents is a qualified teacher, not necessarily the one with day-to-day responsibility for home educating. Almost half the parents have no post-school education. A quarter of the families had other children in school besides the ones they were educating at home.

THE RESEARCH

The research is necessarily exploratory. Very little is known about the way parents go about educating their children at home. Very little, too, is known about individualized teaching or informal learning. The point of the research is to gain insights into these aspects of teaching and learning at home. The appropriate database is therefore qualitative and, as will become evident, fulfils nearly all the following criteria specified in Cobb and Hagemaster's (1987) definition of qualitative research:

- there is attention to the social context in which events occur and have meaning;
- there is an emphasis on understanding from the point of view of the participants in it;
- the approach is primarily inductive;
- major collection techniques include interviewing, participant observation, examination of personal documents;
- procedures and tools for data gathering are subject to ongoing revision in the field situation;
- the concern is primarily with discovery and description;
- hypotheses are usually developed during the research, rather than a priori;
- analysis is presented for the most part in narrative rather than numerical form.

Interviews

It was left to the family to decide who should be at the interview. The parent with the main, day-to-day responsibility for home education was always present and, on occasion, his or her partner or some other relative or friend. Children were sometimes present, or at least 'around' in which case they sometimes contributed. Interviews generally lasted between one and two hours. Parents were told, beforehand, they would be sent a copy of the interview transcript which they could add to, change, edit or delete as they wished. They were thus assured they could reflect on what they had said at the interview and discuss the transcript with partners and/or children. It also meant they could be sure that their experiences would be fully and accurately presented. Incidentally, there was a minor drawback with this procedure; a few parents changed colloquialisms and grammatical abbreviations to make the transcript more 'presentable'. This detracted from the greater sense of immediacy conveyed by the spoken word, not to mention the loss of some very colourful expressions!

I conducted all the interviews, which were almost completely open-ended. Parents were asked first to describe what led them to decide to educate their children at home. Apart from helping to establish rapport and a relaxed ambience (this is a story all home educators are keen to relate), it also helped to orient parents to the main focus of the interview, how their children learned at home. Some parents needed no further prompting and went on to describe how they went about their task in detail. If they did not they were simply asked to describe, in detail, a typical week, a typical day, how literacy was taught and developed and to talk about social aspects of home education. It needs to be mentioned that this protocol did not become standard until after the first twenty or so interviews, the original intention having being to use the interviews mainly as a means of establishing a good rapport prior to requesting permission to observe learning in the home.

Sound recording of interviews was considered and rejected, mainly for the following reasons. First and foremost, while recording may be essential when every word needs to be captured, it is less useful if one wants information based on thoughtful reflection. Second, it is inhibiting, especially for a group of people who, from their point of view, are being asked to explain their competence as educators. Third, when notes are taken there are short breaks when the interviewer is writing which allow for marshalling of thoughts, reflection and recall. In some instances, parents were being asked to recall how they thought and what they did years previously. Fourth, it would have taken parents an inordinate amount of time to edit the transcript of a recorded interview.

The interview transcripts were analysed in order to identify themes and common approaches. In some instances, individualistic approaches to teaching and learning are described on the basis that all the families are pioneers, creatively seeking out what works best in light of their particular circumstances.

Observations

The original intention of the research had been to conduct a small-scale study based on observations of education at home and, during the first phase of the study, a number were carried out. But they were intrusive. It is not easy to have someone in your kitchen watching you teach your children. Teachers, especially new ones, find observation stressful; inspections are highly stressful and dreaded. Parents who, in a very real sense, are challenging the educational establishment, though few would see it like this, are even more concerned about being observed. This is not to say that observing home education is out of the question. But it would require a long-term strategy in which the observer spends a considerable amount of time with each family in order to gain acceptance and, not least, to capture learning which can take place from first thing in the morning to last thing at night.

The next step was to invite parents, instead, to record or describe examples of children's learning themselves. With a few exceptions this did not work out either, partly because they were unsure of what was required (in spite of a briefing session and detailed written guidelines) and partly because it was too time-consuming.

Some observations, which were recorded, are included by way of illustration. Just one parent became very enthusiastic about recording her child's learning which she continued to do over a number of years. A small part of her journal serves as the basis for the detailed analysis of informal learning in Chapter 8.

Chapter 2

Theoretical Background I:
Teaching Children Individually[1]

The mind of every individual is unique and enormously complex. It is only through purposeful dialogue that a teacher (parent, mentor, etc.) can be certain of starting from where the learner is at, appreciate what is to be learned from the learner's point of view, monitor progress in understanding, deal with problems as and when they arise, and continually adjust and readjust teaching strategies in line with progress towards mastery, understanding or enlightenment.

Socrates was probably the first recorded teacher to teach through dialogue with each of his students. The Socratic method entails asking questions, each question contingent on the answer to the previous one. Quintilian, the Roman philosopher, was one of the first to bring attention to individual differences.

> The skilled teacher, when a pupil is entrusted to his care, will first of all seek to discover his ability and natural disposition [and will] next observe how the mind of his pupil is to be handled . . . for in this respect there is an unbelievable variety, and types of mind are no less numerous than types of body. (In Lawrence, 1970, p. 43)

This very simple idea, that the nub of teaching should take account of individual differences and consist of a dynamic interaction between the teacher and learner, has been reiterated by philosophers and educators ever since. Even the arch-empiricist, John Locke, argued that

> Each man's mind has some peculiarity, as well as his face, that distinguishes him from all others and there are possibly scarce two children who can be conducted by exactly the same method. (In Sheasgreen, 1986, p. 73)

Rousseau is generally regarded as the most influential exponent of individualized teaching:

> Each mind has a form of its own in accordance with which it must be directed; and for the success of the teacher's efforts it is important that it should be directed in accordance with this form and no other. I cannot too strongly urge the tutor to adapt his instances to the capacity of his scholar. (In Lawrence, 1970, p. 158)

John Dewey, the father of modern educational philosophy, stood firmly in this tradition.

Without insight into the psychological structure and activities of the individual, the educative process will therefore be haphazard and arbitrary. (In Dworkin, 1959, p. 20)

Here Dewey was referring to developments in mainstream psychology in the late nineteenth and early twentieth centuries, especially research into individual differences in perception, motivation, ability and aptitude. He went even further.

The teacher must be alive to all forms of bodily expression of mental condition – puzzlement, boredom, mastery, the dawn of an idea, feigned attention, tendency to show off, to dominate discussion because of egotism, etc. – as well as sensitive to the meaning of all expression in words. He must be aware not only of their meaning, but of their meaning as indicative of the state of mind of the pupil, his degree of observation and comprehension. (Dewey, 1933, p. 274)

Dewey differed from earlier philosophers because he actually tried to put what he called his Pedagogic Creed into practice, though the school in which he did so was rather special and had very little in common with conventional schools of the time ... or since! Dewey's school was located on the campus at the University of Chicago, mainly attended by children of academic staff. There were 140 children taught by 25 full-time teachers and ten part-time assistants and, no doubt, numerous university graduate students (Garforth, 1966). School policy clearly translated Dewey's philosophy into practice:

Individual attention is secured by small groupings of children and a large number of teachers (*ibid.*, p. 65) ... It is expected that the teacher will give attention to the specific powers and deficiencies of each child, so that individual capacities will be brought out, and individual limitations made good (p. 74).

So far then we have a clear educational philosophy based on individualized teaching, but one which could only be put into practice by tutors of children of the wealthy and by teachers in extremely well-endowed schools such as Dewey's.

ATTEMPTING TO INDIVIDUALIZE TEACHING IN THE CLASSROOM

Since the earliest times, with few exceptions, classroom teaching consisted of rote learning and drill. This suited the curriculum which consisted mainly of learning the classics and scriptures by heart. If philosophers espoused individualized teaching, very few schools practised it, or needed to. There was little point in adapting to individual children. The development of universal education in the nineteenth century continued this tradition except that great care was taken to limit the amount of learning, even by these methods.

If the lower orders were going to be educated, their social superiors had to ensure that the nature and content of the education offered were carefully controlled ... intellectual instruction, therefore had to be subordinated to the regulation of the thoughts and habits of the children by the doctrines and precepts of revealed religion. (Hurt, 1979, p. 112)

The teaching methods used admirably realized the early aims of universal education. Theory and practice were securely in accord. However, towards the end of the nineteenth century there was increasing parental and political pressure for a better education for all children. Under the influence of writers such as Dewey, and the emerging psychological interest in children embodied in the Child Study Movement, many educators were pressing for a radical change in both curriculum and pedagogy.

Edmund Holmes, an HM Inspector of Schools, in a very influential book, *What Is and What Might Be*, written after he retired, lamented the all-prevailing drudgery in the schools he had visited (Holmes, 1919).

Dewey and his disciples provided a fresh pedagogical philosophy, based on a much broader curriculum and individualized teaching. Giving greater breadth to the curriculum posed few difficulties. But no one suggested how to teach individual children in classes of 30-plus, taught by a single teacher. However, the disciples of individualized teaching were very persuasive, as a 1927 government *Handbook of Suggestions for Teachers* illustrates.

> The characteristic note of recent educational doctrine or practice has been the insistence on the importance of the individual as distinct from the class. (Board of Education, 1927, p. 53)

The result was that generations of teachers were exhorted to individualize their teaching. The Plowden Report (1967) strongly asserted that

> Individual differences between children of the same age are so great that any class, however homogeneous it seems, must always be treated as a body of children needing individual and different attention. (p. 25)

The Report conceded that demands on teachers would be 'frighteningly high' (p. 311), but argued that teachers would be able to cope if they combined individual, group and class work, supplementing knowledge of individual children by discussions with parents. They asserted, without a shred of supporting evidence, that this could be achieved provided class sizes did not exceed 30.

The Plowden Report put an official seal of approval on what teachers had been trained to do for decades, even though the first thing newly qualified teachers did was abandon what they had been taught, instead acquiring the disciplinary, managerial and 'whole class' teaching skills which the realities of school demanded.

The ORACLE study, the first major observational study of primary school classrooms, was undertaken to find out how far the Plowden prescriptions had been put into practice (Galton *et al.*, 1980). They found that teachers actually did individualize their teaching, though not in the way the Plowden Report had envisaged. There was a great deal of interaction with individual pupils, so from the teacher's point of view the teaching was individualized. However, each pupil received very little individual attention, an average of 2.3 per cent of lesson time, and even that was 'overwhelmingly factual and managerial' (p. 157). A great deal of learning was individualized, but only in the sense that children spent three-quarters of lesson time working on their own, at their own rate. The questioning and exploratory nature of learning in which the teacher interacts with individual children, in a probing, questioning and guiding sense, the hallmark of individualized teaching, was, paradoxically, only found in whole-class 'chalk and talk' teaching.

> In this situation the teacher does not have to concentrate her mind and her activity on the management of thirty individualized tasks, but on one only, the subject matter under discussion. (p. 158)

Bennett *et al.* (1984) carried out detailed analyses of teacher–pupil interaction, supplemented by pupil and teacher interviews, and came to broadly similar conclusions. They found that teachers, even experienced and 'above-average' teachers who subscribed to a philosophy of individualized teaching, did not practise it in the way that Dewey or Plowden envisaged. They noted that less than half the tasks allocated to pupils in the upper infant school were found to be matched to their abilities, highly unlikely if the teachers were genuinely interacting with pupils on an individual basis. Moreover, the level of matching deteriorated further after the children moved up to the junior school where less than one-third of the tasks were matched.

As the authors point out, poor matching must be a consequence of poor diagnosis.

> The teachers did not diagnose. They reacted to the product of a child's task performance rather than to the processes or strategies deployed in attaining the product. Thus procedural matters, such as taking the child through the rules of carrying numbers or providing spellings, predominated, rather than diagnosis of the nature of the child's difficulty. (p. 217)

The researchers then went on to train these teachers in the use of individual diagnostic techniques. Even then the teachers were unable to put into practice what they had learned. The (blindingly obvious) reason for this, according to the authors, was that classroom management constraints simply did not allow sustained interaction with any of the children.

There have since been numerous attempts to understand how individual children conceive learning tasks and the strategies they employ in tackling them. While these provide some interesting insights into individual processes of learning, they only serve to underline the futility of trying to cater for them in the conventional classroom. Here is one example which fulfils the first requirement of individualized teaching – to listen intently to the learner. An 11-year-old boy is encouraged to talk about a test item administered by the Assessment and Performance Unit. The researchers were trying to find out why pupils find certain test items difficult (Joffe and Foxman, 1989).

> Jason (reading the question out aloud to the investigator) 'Put these decimals in order of size, smallest first: 0.064, 0.35, 0.64, 1.1 [says numbers] Zero point zero six four, zero point three five, zero point six four, one point one. This looks a bit tricky at first ... it looks like a catch but it's not, I don't think, because 1.1 will go first because it's got a one at the start instead of a zero; so that will go highest 'cause I'm working my way down. Then the second ... this is a bit tricky the second for me. I think they'd both share second, because it's got 0.64 and 0.064 and I don't think that that first zero after the point doesn't sort of matter ... I think they'd share the same place ... But there again I think that zero might mean zero a bit, sort of a bit down from 0.64 ... as an answer they'd be joint second and then as a last one it would be 0.35 'cause that is lower than 0.64 and 1.1.' (p. 20)

The authors cite this example to demonstrate that it is essential, if pedagogy is not to be meaningless, to listen to the learner's cognitions concerning his or her task. The next step is also obvious, that the listener engage Jason in conversation to try and negotiate how best to proceed. This is the truly pedagogical element. Joffe and Foxman rightly suggest, in the light of this and other examples from their research, that more discussion between individual pupils and teachers is fundamental to any real improvement in the quality of learning. What they do not do is to suggest how this can be achieved in the classroom. In fact we only get this far with Jason because someone is available who is free from the demands of classroom management.

Bennett *et al.* (1984) describe and analyse at length (across three pages) the problem that a single child, Helen, had with dealing with change from shopping. The teacher partly understood Helen's problem, but had no time to pursue it. The researcher, who was recording Helen's progress, talked at length with her, probing a good deal further into the nature of her difficulty. This made it possible to establish that Helen understood the concept of 'change' but had somehow misunderstood what was expected of her. Even though Helen's problem was highlighted it was still left unsolved.

Rowland (1984), a practising teacher, arranged to spend a year working with individual and small groups of children ... but it had to be in someone else's classroom!

> [the class teacher] ... took responsibility for the overall management of the class, its curriculum, normal assessment procedures and so forth. This left me free, during class sessions, to focus attention on individuals or groups of children for considerable lengths of time. (p. 8)

He describes his interaction with some of the children in great detail. Following on from his experiences, Rowland writes of the pedagogical necessity of building what he calls a 'conversational relationship' in which new ideas and alternative perspectives are suggested to individual pupils, enabling them to reflect on and sometimes reinterpret what they learn. In one example he encourages a pupil, Dean, to develop his own system of taxonomy. In another he refers to two pupils, David and Greg, whom he has inspired to learn the Fibonacci number series. Rowland has to be on hand all the time while they are becoming acquainted with the series, until each, after different intervals, begins to take control and to develop different series of his own, all of this happening within the context of the 'conversational relationship' he has established with them.

These examples are interesting for two reasons. First, they demonstrate that when we want to talk about the process of learning, as opposed to its product, it is impossible to get away from dealing with individuals whose learning strategies are unique to themselves. A passing remark to a child, which is all most teachers have time for, is not enough. It is only through discussion and patient negotiation that it is possible to get an insight into the task as it is perceived by the learner.

Second, the researchers who carried out the studies are reluctant to spell out the implications of their research. Bennett *et al.* (1984) talk of the need to reconceptualize the classroom to allow for more interaction between teacher and pupil, but they do not specify how it can be done. Joffe and Foxman (1989) plead for more discussion between teacher and individual child without prescribing how it is to be achieved. Rowland (1984) does not explain how he intends to carry out conversational relationships he has developed with individual children when he returns to his own classroom. Their reluctance to spell out the consequences of their research is understandable. It is simply impossible to get away from the problem of what to do with the rest of the class.

EXPERIMENTAL STUDIES IN SMALL GROUP, ADULT–CHILD AND PEER TUTORING

If teachers do not have time to interact at length with individual children in the normal course of teaching, is it possible to do so in small group teaching? Wertsch and Kanner (1992) review a number of studies in which teachers deliberately fostered a conversational relationship, even if narrowly conceived. For example, they cite a study by

Palinscar and Brown (1986) in which children who were poor readers were taught in small groups to improve their literacy skills. They worked interactively with the teacher who used the strategies of summarizing, questioning, clarifying and predicting during 20 daily half-hour sessions. The results of this and other similar studies lead Wertsch and Kanner to suggest three factors which contribute to their success. First, the teachers have to come into contact with individual students in order to assess each one's existing level of knowledge; second, the pupil must participate actively in pupil–teacher interaction; third, the pupil must be encouraged to move towards independence, from what they call intermental to an intramental form of functioning. This latter point is in keeping with Vygotskian theory, in which new learning emerges from shared (conversational) knowledge into individual knowledge. At the practical level the study shows that individualized teaching in small groups is feasible.

The idea of using children as tutors stems from the monitorial system introduced in the early nineteenth century. Its appeal at the time was undeniable. It was argued that one teacher could drill ten children who would in turn drill another ten and so on, so that only a single teacher might be required for a thousand children. Not even the most 'back-to-basics' guru would go this far today. But the use of pupils to teach other pupils has many attractions. Reviews of the considerable body of research into peer and cross-age tutoring are generally favourable (Allen, 1976; Cohen *et al.*, 1982; Limbrick *et al.*, 1985; Sharpley and Sharpley, 1981; Topping, 1988). But nearly all the research to date has focused on outcomes rather than processes (Topping, 1992) so that little is known about how far individualized teaching and dialogue contribute to its success.

Some reservations concerning peer tutoring have been expressed which do impinge on the quality of interaction between tutee and tutor. It seems that while child tutors are very good at choosing the right time to intervene, when the learner is experiencing difficulty, they do not know when to withdraw gradually as the learner gains in competence (Wood, 1992). Peer tutors also tend to concentrate on the concrete, with less regard for conceptual connections, and often just give answers without explanation (Rogoff, 1990). This is not surprising – even some parents do not interact contingently when they help their children with a specific task, as Wood *et al.* (1978) found when they studied the effects of different kinds of parental involvement on young children's learning. They observed 3- to 5-year-old children attempting a construction task. Five levels of parental involvement were identified: (1) general verbal encouragement; (2) specific verbal instruction; (3) assisting in the choice of material; (4) preparing material for assembly; (5) demonstrating an operation. General verbal encouragement was found not to be effective. Specific instruction tended to demoralize the children, so that after encountering failure after failure most would eventually give up. Children taught by demonstration watched what the adult did and were keen to have a try, but when they did, it became clear that they had been unable to take in much of what they had been shown, and once again little progress was made. What they did find was that children taught 'contingently', that is at levels 3 and 4, gradually learned how to do the task. Wood (1988) describes what happens when this type of teaching is used.

> The children who learned the most about the task were exposed to a style of instruction that combined showing and telling in a specific pattern. The mothers of the children who learned most might, for instance, try to suggest or tell the child what to do next, but if he did not understand what was said, perhaps choosing blocks different in size or shape to those she described, his mother might immediately offer more help. She might point to one

of the blocks and say 'This doesn't look quite right. Why not try that one?' When the child succeeded in following a suggestion, however, the mother would step back and let him take more responsibility for what happened next ... By teaching children 'contingently' – that is, by making any help given conditional upon the child's understanding of previous levels of instruction, these mothers ensured that the child was not left alone when he was overwhelmed by the task, and also guaranteed him greater scope for initiative when he showed signs of success. (p. 79)

This study is particularly interesting for two reasons. First, the kinds of instruction found to be ineffective – general verbal encouragement, specific verbal instruction and demonstrating an operation – are routine features of classroom teaching, while individually contingent teaching strategies are not. Perhaps the adults who relied on the ineffective strategies were simply following the modes of teaching which they themselves had experienced in school. Second, the construction task chosen by Wood was deliberately difficult, generally too much so for children under 7 or 8 years of age. Yet the 3- to 5-year-old children who participated in the study were able to master it if they had a mentor whose teaching was dovetailed into their learning.

There are two studies in which adults are compared directly with child tutors, in which adults and peer tutors helped 8- to 9-year-old children solve memory and planning tasks (Ellis and Rogoff, 1982; Radziszewska and Rogoff, 1988). In general the adults were much better able to facilitate learning. They were better able

> ... to orient the children to the task, to provide links between current knowledge and the new situation [while the learners] participated in guided decision making with their roles collaboratively adjusted so that they were involved at a level that was challenging but within reach. (Rogoff, 1990, p. 166)

As in the Wood *et al.* (1978) study, described above, parents are not equally able to help their children learn. The difference between children who performed well and poorly after working with adults related to the extent to which they shared in guided decision making with the adults. Rogoff suggests it is:

> ... social interaction that allows children to take advantage of the bridging, structuring and transferring of responsibility ... processes involved in guided participation. (p. 169)

If, in general, peer tutors do not perform as well as adults, how can the successful outcomes of peer-tutoring research be explained? One possibility is that many successes could simply reflect an increase in 'on task' behaviour, as suggested by Goodlad and Hirst (1990). In a study which did examine process in school-based adult tutoring, pupils between 9 and 13 years of age were taught specific aspects of probability and cartography, either in a class of 30 or in groups of two or three. There were eleven periods of instruction during a three-week block. Overall the results were striking; the mean difference in achievement was of the order of two standard deviations. But conversational interaction between tutor and taught did not play a significant role. The most important distinguishing feature was the increase in time spent 'on task' (Anania, 1983; Bloom, 1984). In keeping with this, Damon (1984) proposes that peer tutoring is best suited for transmitting information and drilling special skills, rather than promoting intellectual growth. So it works better the closer it is to what the monitorial system intended it to be.

If the success of peer tutoring projects in the classroom can be explained simply by an increase in 'on task' behaviour it will remain little more than yet another weapon in the teacher's armoury of strategies for keeping noses to the grindstone.

There are children of school age who do gain a great deal from individualized teaching – those with severe learning difficulties. One of the reasons for this success, it seems, is that because of the daunting learning problems they present, educators have increasingly enlisted parents as partners in their children's education. In the case of severely hearing-impaired children, for example, very few make substantial progress without a great deal of parental input (Reed, 1984).

WHAT IS WRONG WITH CLASSROOM TEACHING?

The argument for individualized teaching will lose its force to the extent that conventional methods of classroom teaching are effective. The amount of research into classroom teaching and learning is awesome. Yet the holy grail, teaching methods that make real and permanent differences to the quality of learning, remains elusive. So-called successes are invariably short-lived. I will focus on four reviews of advances in classroom research in the core areas of reading, writing, maths and science.

Reading

Francis (1985) rightly points out that learning to read cannot be simply regarded as the serial acquisition of mechanical information-processing skills culminating in an efficient code-breaking ability, although the skills are important, as recent research with phonic methods has shown. She argues that something extra is necessary, the application of a child's personal knowledge and problem-solving skills to social contexts concerned with reading.

> The conception of the learner as actively constructing his own knowledge about reading and developing his own learning and reading strategies demands a somewhat different view of the teacher from that of method practitioner and diagnostician. Additionally and centrally he or she becomes a guide and a fellow reader of whatever text is being explored. (p. 12)

Francis is obviously extolling the advantages of individualized teaching. Encouraging parents to read to and with their children has been reported to yield positive results in learning to read for some time, since the pioneering study of Tizard *et al.* (1982). What Francis cannot do is specify exactly how a teacher can go about becoming 'a guide and fellow reader' for 30 children, all at different levels, progressing at different rates and with different interests. Even more so if, on top of this, they are expected to assess and then make use of each child's personal knowledge and personal problem-solving skills. Ironically, especially with regard to the focus of this book, teachers cannot utilize the findings of such research, but parents can!

Writing

Wilkinson (1985) points out that a great deal of progress has been made in the development of the writing curriculum, especially in breaking down the skill of writing into various styles or genres: narrative, descriptive, dialectical, expository, philosophical and poetic. Another approach, according to Wilkinson, has been to establish levels of writing competence, through analyses of samples of pupils' writing: identifying steps involved in the development of writing, analysis of writing skills, assessing performance at different ages, and so on. These kinds of research are undoubtedly very valuable, but they simply do not address the central question of how actually to *teach* writing.

Wilkinson was only able to cite two major studies focused on the actual teaching of writing. In the first of these, carried out in Scottish secondary schools, about half of what the pupils wrote was found to be either copied or dictated. Most teachers expected their pupils to be somehow able to write, rather than to have to teach them the skill. There was also a belief, commonly held, that writing was a general ability they could do little to influence. The second study cited a government report on secondary education, found 'a frequent pattern of rules and essays, drills, exercises, tests' (DES, 1979, cited in Wilkinson, 1985, p. 34). Wilkinson concluded that 'there is a good deal of low level cognitive writing – recording, note taking – going on in secondary schools' (p. 35).

Bennett *et al.* (1984) show that the teaching of writing in the primary school is little better, teachers' overriding concerns being that a piece of writing should have a title, a date, be of an acceptable length and have a minimum of spelling and grammatical errors. Incidentally, they found that children's ability to express themselves in writing, which was not taught, did improve over time, while correct grammar and spelling, which were emphasized, hardly improved at all.

What, according to Wilkinson, is to be done? Very little. He refers to just one study aimed at improving writing ability. It is a study of composing and revision processes undertaken with 16 primary pupils, the outcome of which is the suggestion that the way forward is (wait for it!) to have individual conferences with each child. His simple conclusion is that 'the current depressingly low level of writing skills' can only be improved significantly through individualized teaching. He has no practical proposals which would actually help a classroom teacher. Nor does he suggest how individual conferences for 30 children are to be organized.

Maths

In a review of research on maths teaching, Hart (1985) points out that a great deal of effort has been expended in analysing mathematical tasks and in finding out what children of different ages are capable of solving. Thus, as she says, we now have better insights into conceptual and developmental aspects of the subject. In addition, difficulties in learning maths have been researched through 'the increased use of interviews with children to obtain information on how they solved mathematical problems' (p. 54). Through this type of research, according to Hart, we have come to appreciate that

> misconceptions, intuitive ideas or child methods may form distinctive blocks to a child's understanding [which] must be recognised if the child is to learn what we wish to teach. (p. 54)

Bennett *et al.* (1984) and the CSMS (Concepts in Secondary Maths and Science) team (DES, 1980–82) are among other researchers who have demonstrated individualistic and intuitive methods which children typically use.

The CSMS researchers documented mathematical achievement and errors of 10,000 children aged between 11 and 15 (DES, 1980–82). In general they lamented the low cognitive level of teaching and achievement. They found that half the children in the study had no more than a tenuous and very limited understanding of the number system which they should have acquired in the primary school. In consequence they reason that it is

> impossible to present abstract mathematics to all types of [older] children and expect them to get something out of it. It is much more likely that half the class will ignore what is being said because the base upon which the abstraction can be built does not exist. (CSMS, in Wood, 1988, p. 198).

They argue that teaching must be matched to each individual and recommend a shift away from showing and teaching to 'let us discuss what this means'. By way of example they cite a dialogue with a girl of 14 who is shown a signpost with Grange marked 18 km to the left and Barton 23 km to the right. She is asked how far it is from Grange to Barton. (We will leave aside the 'howler' in the question which assumes there is no other way of travelling between the two places and the fact that road distances are always marked in miles in the UK.)

> Hilary: Oh no, I'm no good at these ... you times those two together don't you? ... No, you can't ... (long pause)
> Interviewer: Imagine standing there and you're looking up at the signpost, OK? Now that way it's 18 kilometres to Grange and that way it's 23 to Barton: we want to know the distance between the two.
> H: 23.
> I: 23?
> H: (long pause) ... I'm not very good at doing kilometres ...
> I: Let's try something else. We're sitting right here, right? Say someone said it was three paces to the window and it was five paces to the window that way ...
> H: You'd add them.
> I: How far from one window to the other?
> H: (Long pause) ... Eight.
> I: Yes, what are you doing?
> H: Adding them!
>
> (CSMS, in Wood, 1988, pp. 194–5)

Science

Driver (1985) summarizes the dilemma facing science teaching, that as we have come to understand the complexities involved in understanding scientific concepts, the differing requirements of individual learners have become more apparent.

> The most recent developments suggest that improving learning outcomes requires ... an insight into individual cognitive processes. (p. 58)

She refers to the well-documented finding, repeatedly verified since the pioneering work of Barnes (1969), that pupils' perceptions of the purpose of science lessons often differ from pupil to pupil as well as between pupils and the teacher. Pupils typically have insufficient prerequisite knowledge or have alternative conceptions of what is required of them which interferes with their learning.

Driver notes, in common with the authors of the ORACLE study (Galton *et al.*, 1980), that the nearest the teacher can get to the kind of teaching which takes account of individual cognitive processes, perceptions and prior knowledge is, paradoxically, when teaching the whole class at the same time.

> If there was any imaginative, analytical, thought-provoking or enquiry-based thinking it was done by the teacher with the whole class. (Sands, quoted by Driver, 1985, p. 61)

She concludes rather pessimistically:

> ... given the minimal conditions necessary for students to remain on task are met, no simple solution to the problem of improving teaching can be put forward. The effects of any given teaching strategy are complex and vary from pupil to pupil ... (Power, cited by Driver, 1985, p. 65)

Clearly, the only real advance in teaching during this century has been in the area of curriculum analysis, providing better conceptuo-developmental insights into the structure of knowledge as faced by the learner. But, as these reviewers recognize, this is not enough, largely because of the distinctive way in which each pupil relates to the curriculum. They all share the belief that there is no sure way forward unless means are found for teachers to interact with pupils at an individual level. But no one suggests how this is to be achieved.

WHERE DO WE GO FROM HERE?

As long as a single teacher has the responsibility for a large number of children, then the time-honoured methods are probably the best. If chalk and talk is used in conjunction with keeping noses to the grindstone, in current argot, whole-class methods in conjunction with classroom management techniques which maximize 'on task' behaviour or Active Learning Time, then we may have arrived at an optimal pedagogy for teaching a large number of children at the same time. Over the last hundred years innumerable educational innovations have been tried but have failed to outlast the enthusiasm of their proponents. So, understandably, in both the UK and Australia, there are government moves to return to an updated version of the classroom as it was in the nineteenth century.

The price is a denial of the fundamental principle that pedagogical quality requires a certain amount of interaction between teacher and individual pupil. One could go further and propose that it is a denial of children's rights not to take seriously their conceptions of the learning material with which they are confronted.

However, it must be acknowledged that all we have so far constitutes little more than persuasive argument. Actual evidence only underlines the impossibility of interacting meaningfully with individual children in the conventional classroom. There is virtually no research into individualized teaching, which is astonishing, given that it has forever been assumed to be the essence of good pedagogy.

Individualized teaching cannot be studied in school because it rarely occurs there. It is possible to set up experiments, as we have seen, but these are invariably artificial and prey to the flaws inherent in short-term intervention research. The only way to find out more in a setting in which it is routine for a child to be taught individually is to study children who are educated at home.

NOTE

1   The material in this chapter is partly based on an article 'Individualised teaching' published in the *Oxford Review of Education* (Thomas, 1992).

Chapter 3

Theoretical Background II:
Learning in the Early Years[1]

THE ROLE OF SOCIAL CONVERSATION

A different rationale for the study of children educated at home stems from the consideration that nearly all children make an incredible amount of intellectual progress during the first few years of life with little deliberate teaching, simply in the course of everyday living at home. This gives rise to the intriguing question of how far children could continue to learn in this way after reaching school age if they did not go to school.

During the first few years of life children probably experience the richest learning environment they will ever encounter. The amount of knowledge they acquire is phenomenal, about both the culture they are born into and its fundamental intellectual elements. They learn language, a tremendous feat in itself. They acquire the essential building blocks for science, technology, mathematics, literacy and so on. They learn how to deal with their emotions and accumulate a wide range of social skills.

This prodigious amount of learning cannot be accomplished alone. The greater part can only be learned through interaction with and guidance from people who know more, generally parents or carers. Only recently has research begun to describe the vital role of everyday social conversation in learning and development in infancy.

The constructs which emerge from this research serve to highlight why conversational learning, at least in the early years, is so effective. Schaffer (1984) describes how parents facilitate early communication skills through 'dovetailing'. Snow (1977) and Bruner (1983) respectively use the terms 'motherese' and 'scaffolding' to describe how adults provide appropriate linguistic structures which promote language acquisition. Bruner went on to describe pedagogy as an 'extension of conversation' (Bruner, 1990). Wood (1988) uses the term 'contingency' to describe model parental teaching which consists of a sensitive amalgam of showing, telling and knowing when to leave alone. Vygotsky-inspired research into learning in the 'zone of proximal development' shows how the child's grasp of a concept is developed through social interaction with an adult (Rogoff and Wertsch, 1984). Rogoff (1990) goes further, proposing that 'guided participation' within everyday social activities is all that is necessary for normal intellectual development and learning in the early years and that parents or carers do not need to set out deliberately to teach. Tizard and Hughes (1984) coin the phrase 'intellectual search' to characterize how children, as they approach school age, play a very active role in acquiring knowledge and honing their thinking skills through naturally occurring conversation at home, parents providing what Lloyd (1990) calls a 'communicative support system'.

We now know that even newborn infants already have the necessary perceptual and cognitive skills to interact with and learn from their parents from birth, even before. The belief that the neonate experiences the world as 'a blooming, buzzing confusion' has long been superseded. Very soon after birth an infant can distinguish two- from three-dimensional figures, can discriminate levels of brightness with only a 5 per cent difference in luminosity, can track a slow-moving stimulus, can discriminate sounds that differ in loudness, duration, direction and frequency. Infants prefer to look at moderately complex patterns and objects that move. They appear to become bored with prolonged exposure to the same stimulus. By three months infants show a preference for photographs of their mothers to strangers, though once they have habituated to these they prefer to look at strangers, an instance of their eagerness to get on with finding out about the world (Shaffer, 1989; Meadows, 1986; Smith and Cowie, 1988).

Obviously, then, relatively well-advanced cognitive skills are apparent at birth or soon after. The problem from the child's point of view is that, on her own, she can only make very limited use of them whereas most of what is learned about the world in infancy can only be acquired from someone else. Again, newborn infants are well prepared for interaction with their parents. They show a more organized pattern of reaction to speech than to disconnected vowel sounds. At just a few days old a baby has acquired a preference for the mother's voice to that of a stranger. By the time an infant is just a few months old she is able to follow her mother's direction of gaze even if it means turning around to look at something behind her (Butterworth and Cochran, 1980). Therefore she is able to attend to those things her mother wants to draw her attention to, an essential early learning skill.

Parents play their part too. As if by instinct, they strive to communicate socially with their children from birth. They seem to want to train their babies to interact, even interpreting burps, farts and other random noises and movements as intentional forms of communication, and responding accordingly. Just as her baby follows her direction of gaze, so does a mother follow her baby's focus of attention as a basis for topics of conversation (Rogers, 1985).

An important aspect of interaction is turn-taking. Even when a very young infant is feeding, from either breast or bottle, there is a kind of 'dialogue' apparent. When the infant is sucking the mother is inactive but during pauses between sucking she moves, fondles and talks to her. A pattern of turn-taking, essential for later social interaction and learning, becomes established (Snow, 1977). Moreover, the infant is not a passive participant in turn-taking. Both mother and child equally contribute. In a study of mutual gaze patterns of 12-month-old infants, for example, nearly all looks the infant and the mother directed at each other were of less than two seconds' duration. What is significant from our point of view though is the integration of these looking patterns and the speed at which they are synchronized to a highly sophisticated level of interaction, each constantly monitoring the other and adapting their own behaviour accordingly (Schaffer, 1977). These are just a few examples of numerous studies on early infant development which illustrate how quickly mothers and infants develop highly sophisticated interaction patterns which are essential for the child's learning.

As the child begins to acquire language, the dovetailing (and pedagogical) role of the mother in facilitating intellectual progress, here expanding on the child's language, becomes more obvious:

> Mother: (picks up cup of coffee)
> Child: Hot
> Mother: Hot, hot! Ooh, it's hot!
> Child: Tea
> Mother: No, it's not tea. It's coffee
> Child: Coffee
> Mother: It's lovely. Mmm. Coffee's not nice for you. You're having your dinner now.
> (Snow, in Smith and Cowie, 1988, p. 245)

In naturally occurring everyday social situations and without being conscious of doing so, the mother provides the child with 'next stage' models of language structure, based on those that the child has already mastered. It is precisely because it is one-to-one that the 'teacher' can start from where the 'learner' is at.

An interesting feature of language acquisition is that although all the native speakers of a language end up with more or less the same grammatical and syntactical structures, the route by which they get there seems to differ from child to child, linguists having failed to discover a set of rules which can predict the course of language acquisition (Crystal, 1976). It follows that the 'next stage' models which parents provide for their infants must to some extent reflect this uniqueness. The mother's talk has to be contingent on what the child says. In the sample of child–mother conversation above, it is the nature of the child's utterance which determines the mother's response. She has no predetermined language teaching programme. She simply responds in a socially appropriate way, at the same time providing a 'next stage' cognitive-linguistic model for the child. In fact, direct attempts to teach grammatical structures are generally ineffective (Brown and Bellugi, 1964). The fact that virtually all children master the structure of the language to which they are exposed means that this naturally occurring pedagogy, uniquely adapted to each child, is optimal.

The well-known research by Tizard and Hughes (1984) provides some fascinating insights into how young children continue to learn within the context of naturally occurring social conversation. They describe learning which spontaneously occurs between mothers and their 3- to 4-year-old children. The study is of particular interest because learning at home is compared with learning in a nursery (preschool) class which the children attended on a half-time basis.

As might be expected, there was much more adult–child talk at home than in school, but the authors were surprised to find that the home conversations were of a much higher quality. Some examples they quote extend over pages. In general they found that

> At home children discussed topics like work, the family, birth, growing up and death ... about things they had done together in the past, and plans for the future; they puzzled over such diverse topics as the shape of roofs and chairs, the nature of Father Christmas and whether the queen wears curlers in bed ... [but at school] ... the richness, depth and variety which characterised the home conversations were sadly missing. So too was the sense of intellectual struggle, and of the real attempts to communicate being made on both

sides. The questioning, puzzling child we were so taken with at home was gone ... conversations with adults were mainly restricted to answering questions rather than asking them, or taking part in minimal exchanges about the whereabouts of other children and play material. (pp. 8–9)

On the surface, adult–child conversation at home can appear desultory. But on closer analysis, as Tizard and Hughes point out, it is clear just how much it must contribute to learning. For example, by sharing past experiences and looking forward to future ones, children gained familiarity with the corresponding tenses, which rarely featured in their school conversations. At home, too, there was greater opportunity to initiate conversation than was possible in school where the teachers had to stem the flow of questions because children were only interested in the ones they wanted to ask and got bored when everyone else started to ask theirs. Moreover, a typical teacher strategy was to focus on extracting a predetermined 'correct' answer, often without any real learning occurring. They give an example of a child who takes a piece of card to her teacher and asks:

Child: Can you cut that in half? Cut it in half?
(The teacher asks the child to go to the cupboard to get the scissors. When the child returns she asks her where she wants the paper to be cut. Then she cuts it in half as requested by the child)
Teacher: What have I done if I've cut it down the middle?
C: Two pieces.
T: I've cut it in ... ?
C: [No reply]
T: What have I done?
C: [No reply]
T: Do you know? (Child shakes head)
Other child: Two.
T: Yes, I've cut it in two. But, I wonder, can you think?
C: In the middle.
T: I've cut it in the middle ... I've cut it in half! ...

(p. 194)

At home the children also had many more opportunities for what Tizard and Hughes called 'intellectual search' in which children pursue a line of interest through persistent questioning or over a period of time, dropping and picking up topics, allowing time for reflection in between. Space does not allow justice to be done to Tizard and Hughes' description of this and other forms of learning at home. But by way of illustration here is just one highly truncated example.

Penny's mother had promised to buy her a doll's ballerina outfit for her next birthday and Penny was thinking through the implications of this promise. Knowing that she would not be going with her mother to get it she reasoned that someone would have to look after her. In the conversation which follows her mother says that she will probably buy it when Penny is at school and then suggests, to Penny's excitement, that she might have it for Christmas, which is much sooner. Penny reasons she'll 'have to go in his house and ask him'. Her mother suggests asking Father Christmas in the shops around Christmas time.
[Following the conversation there is an interval during which they talk about something else. Then Penny returns to the topic ...]
Penny: Does Father Christmas ... give me ... does Father Christmas say 'No' if he hasn't got a ... hasn't got a ... dancellina one?
Mother: Well, he does usually have those things.
Penny: Will you ask him?
Mother: We'll do what you did last year and write a letter to him. Remember?

Penny: And what will he say if I write a letter to him?
Mother: He'll say, 'This looks a nice letter, I'll see what I can get. She wants a dancer's
  outfit'.
Penny: He won't know my name.
Mother: He will if you put your name on the bottom.

(pp. 115–16)

This clearly illustrates Penny's 'intellectual search'. In keeping with a great deal of recent research on the intellectual development of young children, she is logical and consistent in her quest for understanding. Her halting expression is itself a well-known feature of intellectual struggle; the researchers found her to be highly articulate, as were most children in their study, regardless of social background.

In the previous chapter we noted that not all adults are equally able to promote their children's learning when the children are given a specific task and the onus is on the parents to teach them. Those who were successful, according to Rogoff (1990) and Wood *et al.* (1978), used strategies similar to those described by Tizard and Hughes (1984) as opposed to the less successful, who used more direct teaching methods. It seems that parents may be better teachers when they don't know they are teaching.

There is virtually no research on informal learning with older children, of school age, neither at home nor in school.

CAN CHILDREN LEARN DURING THEIR SCHOOL YEARS AS AN EXTENSION OF THE WAY THEY LEARNED IN INFANCY?

An intriguing question, which must by now be apparent, is how far children might continue to learn informally, in the manner described by Tizard and Hughes for example, after reaching school age. There is certainly anecdotal evidence which suggests they can, provided by parents who found home education did not turn out quite as they expected, for example:

> In September, equipped with desks, blackboard, books, pens – just like a real school – I proceeded to 'educate' my children. By the end of the day we were all verging on a nervous breakdown ... In two years of home education we have changed, evolved. We sold the blackboard and the desks ... Of course we do maths and English, discuss history, look at maps, talk about the world ... but again it's mainly practical work or discussion. (Webb, 1990, p. 126)

A great deal of this kind of informal learning obviously goes unnoticed, as it does with early learning – unless someone makes a point of recording it. This is simply because it is naturally occurring, largely social conversation in which the pedagogical element simply goes unnoticed. Another home educating parent describes what happened in just one morning.

> Drawing and writing, looked at books of birds, books of Grey Rabbit, elephant pictures of man and lady that lived with elephants for some years, sewing buttonholes, dressing up dolls, bicycle ride. Colours out of doors and changes. Saw a heron in a ditch just close to us. Explored the depths of puddles. Played fairies under the trees and continued the fantasy as we walked home. Counting the curtain rings. Talked about 'half'. Joey helped me to grate fruit and chop nuts for muesli ... long walk with dog and found some toadstools to look up. Radio – Medicine Now ... Jessie crying for a real baby of her own. Talked about babies and age and death and a broken pelvis, cremation and burials ... (Bendell, 1987, p. 121)

THE ROLE OF INDIVIDUALIZED TEACHING AND SOCIAL CONVERSATION IN THE ACCELERATED DEVELOPMENT OF LEARNING IN THE EARLY YEARS

While everyday conversation is essential for normal learning in the early years, it is what happens when conversational learning is deliberately extended that strikingly demonstrates its pedagogical potential. In a review of a large number of studies of accelerated learning, Fowler (1990) concludes that language development and general verbal ability can be accelerated from whatever baseline, equally for children from impoverished as well as from advantaged backgrounds. In one of the studies, the progress of infants taught intensively by their parents was monitored from the age of five months. The effects were marked and long-lasting, still present when the children were 5 years old. The success of the programme was attributed to 'adult language mediated activity [which] appears to function as the chief agent of verbal–abstract mental development during infancy' (p. 194).

Rogoff (1990) cites two studies in which dialogue was used to accelerate conceptual learning in the early years. In the first, mothers were encouraged to use appropriate dialogue, while reading to their 3-year-old children, to facilitate the learning of taxonomic labels. The children who participated in this more directed form of dialogue advanced their knowledge of taxonomy significantly more than those children who did not (Adams, 1987). In the second, Heber (1981) found that dialogue led to a significant improvement in understanding seriation for 5- and 6-year-old children when compared with direct, one-way teaching.

Conversational learning also seems to play a major role in the early origins of giftedness. Howe (1990) demolishes the popular belief that gifted children are born that way. Following a review of a large body of research into the origins of giftedness, he asserts that ' ... the majority of people are born capable of acquiring impressive levels of expertise in most spheres of competence' (p. 4). With regard to conversational learning:

> One especially important finding is that the appropriateness of the speech that is directed to the child is more crucial than the sheer amount of it. The most effective kinds of language teaching occur when an adult and a child are together in a one-to-one situation, and the adult knows what is momentarily engaging the child's attention. (p. 19)

It should come as no surprise to learn that the parents of most child prodigies devoted themselves to their children's education from the earliest years (Bloom, 1985; Feldman with Goldsmith, 1986). As these children grew older they continued to enjoy personal contact with mentors or models (usually relatives or teachers) 'who directly guided, discussed, furnished resources or otherwise interacted with them in intellectually stimulating ways' (Fowler, 1990, p. 199). Similarly, Sosniak (1990), in a retrospective study of twenty outstanding young people, found that as young children 'they learned a good deal in informal ways about knowledge and skills associated with the activities in which they would eventually excel' (p. 154).

Taniuchi (1982) describes the case of a prodigy, Winifred Stoner. The following is a sample of her achievements:

> In her third year she could spell anything requested of her by guests, and she began to write poetry. At four years old she was awarded a diploma in Esperanto. By this age also, she was able to speak and write poetry in English, Esperanto, Latin, French and Spanish. By twelve

years she was the author of numerous published stories and poems, as well as several book-length collections.

What seems to have been important for her phenomenal progress was simply the amount of interaction the child had with her mother.

> From the time Winifred became six weeks old, Mrs. Stoner spent a large part of her day as her daughter's teacher/play companion.

I do not want to advocate hothousing or the deliberate creation of prodigies. The intention is simply to illustrate the pedagogical potential of adult–child informal social interaction.

SUMMARY OF THIS AND THE PRECEDING CHAPTER

Philosophical inquiry points to the power of individualized teaching. Education research confirms this but points to the futility of trying to individualize teaching in the classroom. Developmental psychology points to the potency of informal, mainly conversational learning in the early years. The fascinating question that arises is how far older children can learn in this way after they reach the age at which they would normally start school. The only way to find out more about individualized teaching and informal learning is to study children educated at home.

NOTE

1 The material in this chapter is partly based on an article 'Conversational learning' published in the *Oxford Review of Education* (Thomas, 1994).

Chapter 4

Why Do Parents Choose to Educate Their Children at Home?

Schooling is embedded in the culture. It is where children go to become educated. Starting school is a major milestone in nearly every child's life. The decision not to send a child to school or to withdraw one from school is therefore a momentous one. It is also very radical in the sense that it challenges nearly two centuries of accumulated professional wisdom and research which purportedly authenticate the value of education in school.

Understandably, parents considering home education need to ask themselves many very searching questions. Might they be depriving their children of a proper education? Will they be able to provide a standard of education equivalent to a professional teacher with four years' university training? Will they be able to motivate their children to learn at home? How will they go about it? What if the children refuse to learn? Will the authorities make it difficult? What about inspections? What of social development? Will their children be deprived of friends and isolated from the real world? Will they be able to fit into society when they are older? Or back into school if they return? How will they and their children deal with disapproval from other members of the family and friends? What about the loss of a potential family income? What of personal development and career prospects for the parent (nearly always the mother) who has the main day-to-day responsibility for home education? The list could go on.

Little is known of the reasons which prompt parents to educate their children at home. In the United States, Van Galen (1991), based on a study of 23 families, carried out partly in a home educating Christian academy, proposed two general classes of home educators, Ideologues (mainly Christian) and Pedagogues, people who are not so much opposed to what school is trying to achieve, but who believe they can do a better job. A British study of 20 families found that parents were influenced by reading alternative educational literature by writers such as John Holt and A. S. Neill, conflict between home and school values and specific problems, e.g. bullying and special needs (Webb, 1990). A study of 21 families carried out in Scotland by Paterson (1995) found dissatisfaction with or problems encountered in school were the main reasons, though the decision was generally based on more complex considerations.

The families in the present study fell into two fairly equal groups, those whose children had never been to school (45) and those who withdrew their children from school (55). They ranged from those who were predisposed to educate their children at home from birth (and before) to those who would never have given a thought to home education and withdrew their children from school only as a last resort.

No major differences emerged between the two countries although there may have been a greater awareness of alternatives to conventional schooling in Australia where Distance Education for children living in remote areas features in the national consciousness.

Table 4.1 presents an overall picture of the reasons which contributed to the parents' decision to educate their children at home, garnered from the qualitative data. It is meant only as a rough guide, to provide a backcloth to the more appropriate qualitative analysis which follows. It needs to be underlined and borne in mind throughout the chapter that the reasoning behind the decision was often complex and sometimes taken only after a great deal of deliberation, as will become evident in the qualitative analysis.

Table 4.1   *What influences parents to educate their children at home?*

(a) *Children who did not start school*	(n = 45)	(%)
Media, reading about home education, meeting other home educators	38	(84)
Perceptions of academic and social limitations of schooling	20	(44)
Viewing home education as a continuation when children reach school age	10	(22)
Influenced by having taken an older child out of school	6	(13)
Christian values	5	(11)
Other	11	(24)
(b) *Children withdrawn from school*	(n = 55)	
Media, reading about home education, meeting other home educators	29	(53)
Child's dislike of school	24	(44)
Bullying (including two instances of sexual harassment)	17	(31)
Belief that child would achieve more out of school	15	(27)
Learning difficulties in school	8	(15)
Dissatisfaction with general school values	7	(13)
School does not embody Christian values	6	(11)
Misbehaviour (in school, or at home and attributed to school)	8	(15)
Other	16	(29)

PARENTS WHO OPT FOR HOME EDUCATION FROM THE OUTSET

Families who opted for home education from the beginning were likely to be influenced by one or more of the following: reading about home education; reading more general alternative educational literature; encounters with home educating families; their own experience of schooling; a gradual realization, as their children approached school age, that they could continue and extend what they were already doing with their children. A few were motivated by religious reasons. There was little emphasis on moral values, but some expressed broader social concerns.

Becoming interested in home education

Reading about education in general and educational alternatives in particular was obviously important, in some instances even before having children.

> I came to EO [Education Otherwise] by a process of default. I looked into all the freeschool alternatives but none were satisfactory. I was also influenced by Holt ... by Tizard, and just sort of continued from there. [68]¹

> Going back about 18 years I read the biography of A. S. Neill. Someone lent me the book. It coloured things though I didn't have children. [22]

> It goes back to when I was 17 and the first job I had and the first book I ever bought, by John Holt – *How Children Learn*. I read it. It didn't mean much but set a precedent for my children. [25]

> It started with *Children on the Hill*. [64]

> I first heard about Home Schooling when I was pregnant ... Dr Moore was being interviewed about his book *Better Late than Early*. It made good sense. We decided then and have collected resources all along. It's just continued. [20]

Meeting home educators could be influential. For some this was the first indication they had of any alternative to school.

> [We] were friendly with two school teachers who were home educating before we even considered having children. It had never crossed my mind. I was fascinated by it. Straightaway I thought I'd be happier than sending them off to school. [12]

> They have never been to school; the decision not to was sparked off by home educating friends ... [71]

> Friends of ours were home educating. At first we were very sceptical. It seemed strange ... [49]

> I met [a home educator] at a jumble sale ... she started telling me about home ed. The more I thought ... So I fell into home ed. [66]

> I first heard about home schooling through a friend who said there were a lot doing it ... [57]

> We came across a home ed. family at a wedding when [she] was very young. [My husband] said if that's what the children are like, he wanted to do it. They were so different. [16]

> I met two people who were home educating. I read everything about home ed. I read oodles of stuff over about eighteen months. [2]

> A friend was home educating his own two children. We decided we would ... Our friend's children were doing so well compared with other children. He was a single parent. His children were bright but not cheeky. [50]

> In the UK I'd seen odd EO notices ... 'Your child does not have to attend school.' I thought this was interesting. I met a friend in the US who was homeschooling six children. I was a school teacher in the US. When I met her it had never occurred to us before. I had never heard of homeschooling when I lived in the States. She's the most unlikely person I've ever met to homeschool. I thought if she can, I can. She was the inspiration. When we came back we looked into all the angles, visited homeschoolers ... [99]

Perceived limitations of schooling

Beliefs about what were perceived to be shortcomings of conventional schooling, especially the lack of individual attention, contributed to the decision not to send children to school.

> Children can learn at their own pace at home ... the teacher can't spend much time with each kid, even though she's a good teacher – there's very little direct contact ... At school a child has very little direct contact with adults and is in constant contact with other children of the same age ... [20]

> My brother's children go to a school with 35 in the class. It's just looking after them. [50]

> You can't have 30 children who all want to do something in the given way the teacher is using. [18]

> [We] see school at an early age as a cheap child care facility. [72]

> School turns people into docile citizens; it is sexist, hierarchical and violent ... Nothing is adapted to the individual child. Children thrive if there's someone who cares about them individually. Teachers are just doing a job, often in a mediocre way. [78]

Social limitations were voiced.

> It defeats the purpose of families to send children to school when you are committed to bringing them up ... The main problem is the social life in school and the peer pressure. [16]

> When I had the children I didn't want to send them to school. It's the system that causes children to go off the rails, not families. [25]

Some were influenced by their own experience of school.

> We have memories of our own schooling where, among other things, competition was used as the main motivator and information was taken in for the purpose of passing exams. [23]

> As a lad I hated school. When I was in school I thought there must be a better way. [33]

> School is a tremendous waste of time; in my twelve years I had very little to show for it; I was deprived of my childhood for little gain. [78]

There was a belief that school did not address real life situations.

> The education system is doing what we think is secondary. It's not for problem solving. We have different views. I don't want to put school down but it's impossible in the school situation to solve any real life questions. [18]

> In school you learn about society from the outside. [22]

A few were dissatisfied with their older children's experience of school and decided not to send younger siblings.

> My reasons for EO stemmed from what school had been like for the other three. It was partly selfish – the thought of another 15 years of dragging myself out of bed, of telling them you'll like it when you get there ... [70]

> I had trouble with my daughters in school. There were constant problems, sometimes but not always with bullying. There was not enough emphasis on the things they should have been doing. When they left the primary school they didn't know their times table. There was a lot of catching up to do. There was no individual attention ... There were a few instances of bullying, tying a rope around her middle and pulling until the rope burned,

pushing children off the kerb. Some of my friends' children had rocks thrown at their heads
... I was thinking of sending the boys to school ... I was absolutely astounded when I found
out the number who did it. I thought 'terrific'. I didn't want to go through the same thing
as I'd done with my daughters. [47]

Religious reasons were mentioned, though many other parents might have shared
the sentiments expressed by the first one, that they had the main responsibility for
educating their children. (The latter two families are included here because they were
not motivated by problems in school.)

As Christians we didn't believe the state has the right to educate before us – we felt such
decisions still belonged to us as parents. [45]

From a Christian viewpoint, the schools were not doing what we wanted. Teachers are
more humanistic with man and not God as the authority. Our authority comes from the
Bible – from Deuteronomy – train your children at all times of day. We thought that if we
are going to be fair dinkum we'd better follow this through. [55]

[My husband] felt very strongly that God said the way to start was to take our own children
out of school. [93]

The notion of education as a continuation of early learning at home

The realization that children make a great deal of intellectual progress at home in the
early years of life was a potent consideration for some parents. As their children
approached school age they could see them progressing quite well at home and felt
little would be gained from sending them to school.

Friends who were teachers encouraged us to let him develop ... When it came to time for
school we didn't approach the school. Our teacher friends said: 'Why send him to school?'
They didn't trash schools – rather, he's doing all right, so why send him? [45]

My reason for keeping her at home was a continuation. Why hand it over to someone else
at that particular time? [24]

We felt there was nothing to lose. Why interrupt something that had been going on from
before the age of 5? We'd have felt different if there'd been part-time school ... Schools
take so much time out of a child's day. So we thought, let's give it a go. [89]

Why is it that 'education' is presumed to start at a certain age? And what is it about
learning, certainly during most of the primary years, that parents suddenly can no longer
provide? [22]

We teach them to walk, talk, feed and dress themselves, all the hard stuff. When that basis
is laid we can't be given credit for teaching them two plus two. [50]

My daughter was 3. She wanted to read. I sat with her, she wanted to. I thought, what a
privilege to teach children (I'm a teacher). So I didn't send her to school. I thought then I
was isolated; it was a bit frightening not being like the others. Then I realized it was very
enriching. As I kept going I grew into it. [41]

When [he] reached school age we just continued; nothing changed. [12]

I was doing a lot with [him]. He's really bright. He takes in any information. We always
talked when we were out. I thought then, if only I could I'd keep it like this. [86]

Gradually coming to the decision to home educate

As mentioned above, while there are some common themes behind the decision to home educate, what led up to it was often quite complex and took place over a considerable period of time. Here are two rather different examples.

> When she was young she was in a playgroup and I thought I can do this at home. Then I went to see a Montessori playgroup but was put off that ... then I thought I didn't like any of the schools. The state system was not appealing and I had no money for a private or community school. It started me thinking. I started investigating; I didn't like what I saw. [She] was reading before she was 4 and the first year at school were all into reading readiness. Also there was peer group pressure and I didn't like the social influences. I read Holt. He seemed to say everything I believed in. I knew a lot of teachers and I read a lot about education. One thing was that I went to a swimming pool and saw the teacher bullying the children ... Up to school age children get moral values and identity from the family. Then they go to school. When they come home they are tired – watch TV – don't interact with parents – see little of them and interaction time is minimal. I thought that teachers' views may be very strong and they cannot be impartial. So I looked around and was not very impressed with what I saw. Hell! I can do better than that. I'll do it for a year and see what happens. It was fine. I did it for another year and got confident. It became a normal thing to do. [54]

> When [he] was born I never felt happy with the idea of sending him to school. My niece, who is 21 now, when she went to kindergarten – it was lovely up to 4. Then she became a different person. All the stuff pouring out of her mouth was not what she was. It had nothing to do with herself. She had become completely polluted. It was like losing her. I felt powerless, being close to her but could do nothing about it. I felt if I had a child I wouldn't want him to go through that. Then, a friend for years, who had a baby after me, was looking at all the possibilities, reading various books. She had Jean Bendell's book *School Is Out*. I was inspired by it, so I joined EO – [he] was 2 ... I also read Holt and re-read Summerhill and Montessori books to know what was available. We had already followed the Doman system. He read at 2½. It was so easy it was ridiculous ... When he reached school age we just continued. [100]

REASONS FOR WITHDRAWING CHILDREN FROM SCHOOL

The distinction between not sending children to school in the first place and withdrawing children from school is not necessarily clear-cut. If children are withdrawn soon after starting school it is reasonable to assume their parents are already predisposed towards home education. What seems to happen is that school reinforces the parents in their views about school and they withdraw them. It is not so much a specific problem which impels them to act, rather general dissatisfaction with what they believe is possible to achieve in any school.

> I realized they weren't learning much at school, so they did maths and spelling before school and book reports and music. This was not very good for relaxing family relationships. So, at the beginning I was not happy with academic standards in school. [10]

> ... it was a combination of me being unhappy as a teacher, then the children were unhappy in school, so it was time to try something else. But I wouldn't have gone to court. I'd have sent them back to school. [5]

> In the first year in school, reception, they reversed everything I'd taught him, to ask questions, to express opinions. He was slotted into a system I didn't approve of. [92]

[My partner] had been reading a lot of philosophy and some educational books, e.g. *The Way It's Spozed To Be* and then especially John Holt. After [our son] started school, he kept on going on about home ed. [76]

[She] went to school up to Grade 2. Then we went to Europe for six months ... When we came back there was no way she was going back to school. That six months opened my eyes to the fact that I could do it and they were happy. Before, when she had gone to school it was because of old friends of ours who were school teachers who had talked us out of [home education]. I felt that they shouldn't go to school at 5 or 6 – it was ludicrous. What made the travelling experience better was incidental learning, just living. Scotland was the best example. [She] was 8 or 9 – castles and Mary, Queen of Scots in particular – she got totally involved in British history and hasn't eased up since – it all comes from that. This kind of learning would take place very naturally if allowed to – you can't pursue the interests of 25 at one time. [28]

However, most who withdrew their children did so because they were having to deal with specific problems in school, including unsatisfactory academic progress, bullying, learning difficulties and disruptive behaviour. These parents possibly represent a new wave of home educators who, ten years earlier, might not have contemplated such a course of action.

Concern that children are not being challenged

A number of parents believed the school failed to recognize their children's ability or potential.

When [she] was in Grade 1 I felt she could achieve more in a different environment and in a different way. I'd felt this for some time. I wasn't disappointed with teachers. She'd been to a Montessori school, but I felt she'd learn more and achieve more in a different setting. [3]

We were fed up with school and heard about home ed. We were fed up with doing [one of the children's] homework for him and having to spend so much time pushing him. He was in Grade 8 at the time ... If I'm going to spend so much time pushing him I might as well do it myself. He was getting good marks but it was Grade 5 level and he wasn't doing anything to earn them. [55]

[He] went [to school] at 6. He knew how to read ... He could also handle money, so he had basic numeracy. He was pleased to finally be a student. Because he didn't need attention she got him to help others. Then she'd send him to the sandpit if he was not helping. When he came home to me he'd ask: 'Why do I have to be in the sandpit all the time?' I asked him what he'd done wrong. Then I asked him to ask the teacher. He was told to go to the sandpit because he could do everything, but for him it was a sentence. I told him to ask the teacher if she could give him something to do. Then it was: 'Why can't I read to the teacher every day?' Then: 'She said I can read so I don't have to read to her.' So he stopped reading. I had nothing against the teacher ... there was no negativity in me. [8]

When she was in school she came home at 3 [o'clock] exhausted. I tried to find out what she'd learned and, amidst the many distractions, I found very little ... [14]

We weren't happy with the school. They'd give him extension work and projects to do on his own. He was above the grade he was in. They wouldn't put him up a grade. So we weren't very happy ... He came out in the middle of 1994. This year he felt he'd like to go back to school, but they wouldn't give him a go in a higher grade ... You do feel angry that his ability is not taken into account. [He] would do what they gave him, but he'd gain no enjoyment out of it. He'd just drag himself through it. [53]

[They both] went to the local school for a year and came out more than a year behind what they were when they went in. [91]

The following parents were so concerned about their children's lack of progress they requested and were vindicated by an independent assessment. They nevertheless decided to take their children out.

In Grade 4 he was performing below his ability. We insisted that a full assessment be done. Although on school report cards his reading was rated below average, the Education Department assessment found that it was in fact years above his age group. His maths ability, although in advance when he began school, was [when he was in] Grade 4, only at Grade 2 level. The assessment team told me if I hadn't taught him to read before school, he would never have learned. By the end of second year High School he was in the top 10 per cent of his year for science, on a national science ability test. But in school he was failing science. [21]

I said he wasn't achieving where he should be. He was well below average and miserable. Their basic reply was: 'What's the hurry?' Then they assessed him and they were stunned. He was in the top half per cent of the population. [48]

Concern that children are falling behind

Dissatisfaction with progress was also expressed by parents who believed their children were being pushed too much in school.

I felt concern at the first parent–teacher interview when the teacher said she was doing well, but I knew she was not. I thought maybe it would be a good idea to repeat Grade 4. [29]

He got angry because he couldn't read ... He wasn't ready to. The school tried to force it. When we felt it was destroying him we pulled him out. [27]

[She] could barely read. The school said her writing was not up to standard and that I should help her. I thought I might as well do it myself. [34]

She was one year ten months behind her reading age. She did a SATs test at 7. They needed '2's to progress. She got a '1' in English and '0's in the rest. So basically she failed. We were told her next school would refuse her, unless we got a lot of work in. They said she'd have to go to a special school and there was a possibility of statementing ... The teacher gave her extra work which we did. It made her stressed. There was no time for herself. At half term there was no improvement. They recommended a one-to-one teacher but couldn't afford one. I decided she'd leave at the end of the year. [98]

Dissatisfaction with progress could be ascribed to a lack of individual attention.

[Our daughter] was in High School, the first one, where she was happy for a short time. It was wonderful at the start and then it started going downhill. We tried changing schools – to a smaller private school where the philosophy was individual teaching in a caring homelike atmosphere ... It sounded ideal. The philosophy of the school was there and it began really well but a lot of the individual attention was more in theory than practice. At home we don't have to move on; we can stay with a topic till we've done it. [Her brother] had lots of trouble in his first school. He was very unhappy, anxious and stressed. There was little understanding on the other side. There was too much pain and we had to do something. He was angry because he had trouble understanding maths and reading. The teachers had very little time to help him. There were no resources and the class was too big. [27]

They all had good reports in the primary school but the teachers didn't have time to make them do things properly – they don't have time to concentrate on the weaknesses of every child in the class. [55]

There were too many people in the class. She had to learn new work without the teacher explaining how to do it. [29]

Bullying

Bullying is endemic in school, though only recently has research pointed to the adverse, sometimes severe, effects it can have on a child's psychological health. While there were instances of severe bullying, most of it was what one parent described as 'low key' and another 'within the normal range of behaviour'. Nevertheless, it was obviously distressing.

[He] was having a rotten time in school where there was a very aggressive bunch of boys. It continued through the school years. He took the brunt of the teasing; he's not aggressive by nature. He was having a raw deal all the time. I persevered hoping there'd be a change, but he came home utterly defeated. I decided to do something. I thought of other schools but I took him out of school ... [His sister] loves school. When we first talked about it her reaction was 'I don't have to give up school, do I?' [9]

He was a school refuser. He'd be awake at night. He'd burst into tears. Strictly speaking, he was bullied, but it was within the range of normal school behaviour, e.g. ganging up. He stood up to it, but it wore him down. [51]

There was mass low-key bullying in school – the classical idea, ganging up on some children ... [He] was always a great reader. If he finished his work he'd read. He stood out a bit different and was teased for reading. The head of the year brought it up and suggested he didn't bring any books. [Finally, my son] said 'If you make me go I'll go and sit on a park bench and come back after school'. I said to the Education Officer 'I don't believe a person should be dragged anywhere'. [90]

I'm not sure why [she] has had problems. Her academic progress is very good. She is very gregarious. But she's frustrated with the 'games' girls play – and they are hierarchical. [31]

[When she started school at ten she] took to it like a duck to water ... In the second year it was fine until there was some bullying by some girls – mental bullying – she didn't say anything but suffered in silence for a time ... Then she started not being well ... She is still out of school and is going to see a psychiatrist next week ... [She] will probably go back in September. She doesn't seem to have a problem as a result of being home educated because she went to the final year of the junior school which she took to like a duck to water. The problem is the secondary school and then not the teachers who think she is wonderful. I think it has a lot to do with bullying, peer pressure from the pack to conform or be left out, and the system. [72]

He got bullied. One child was a monster and 'monstered' him. Once he put a scissors in his face. That was the final straw. He told him 'You'll be dead meat if you tell anyone'. [48]

In September [after the summer holiday] I asked 'Are you OK about going back?' He said 'Yes, after the summer break they'll all be so busy talking about their holidays they won't bother about me'. Unfortunately, this wasn't the case. He was duffed up in the first week, physically and verbally, hauling him round by his coatsleeves, suddenly letting go so he fell down, kicking him in the privates. My gut reaction was – this child can't possibly go back in this school. Before the bullying we'd never thought of home education. [88]

Here is an 8-year-old boy's own account of being bullied.

I always went round with my best friends ... this boy – he was much older than me and he went round with this gang of boys. They kept trying to beat us up, banged our heads on the pipes that came down from the roof. You couldn't play because they always followed us and wanted to fight. The boy who was always bullying us was good [in class] and did his work. He came in [to our class] and threatened to beat us up later. And the dinner ladies didn't do anything ... The Head didn't do much. She said she'd be there when we wanted to see her. When me and my friend went to see her she wasn't there and me and my friend thought she'd be there, but she'd gone for lunch. We had to hide in the toilet sometimes ... [92]

The child in question was not always the victim.

In the junior school he was turning out to be one of the top dogs. I was afraid he might be or about to become a bully and I started not to like him. Although he was 'top dog' he hated going to school. [76]

Sexual harassment

Two parents mentioned their children had been sexually harassed by other children, one in primary and one in secondary school. In neither case did the parents believe the school was taking the problem sufficiently seriously. The first concerns an 8-year-old girl.

There was a major problem at school. We didn't put up with it. A boy in the class was harassing her, not physically. He was sitting next to her. He pulled his pants down ... you show me yours ... We thought the problem had been fixed but he was whispering sexual things to her. Our daughter's behaviour became appalling because of it. She took it out on us. She was totally unable to cope. It was our responsibility to get her out of it. Maybe, if she'd been older ... But at her age she couldn't cope. Another kid might have said 'Get lost!' [46]

The second concerns a 15-year-old girl.

[She] suffered major sexual harassment. I never got to the bottom of it though I took all the right steps to deal with it. At the beginning of the third term she clung to me and didn't want to go to school. I didn't know what to do so I kept her at home. [36]

Behavioural problems in school and at home

Rather surprisingly, children's disruptive classroom behaviour featured among the reasons given for withdrawing them from school.

It was not so much dissatisfaction with school, rather to break a cycle. He is quite a bright kid. Because of the large numbers in the classroom, with the teacher having to teach the majority, he became bored and disruptive and was constantly in trouble ... [13]

They said he was disruptive and out of control. Basically he asked questions they wouldn't answer – they didn't have time. He ended up sitting at a desk on his own. He was a troublemaker because he was bored. [43]

He was in school up to Grade 2. He was a lovely child till he went to school and then he became extremely naughty. Also [his brother] was so naughty he had the teachers crying. [10]

He was disruptive because he was bored. He talked too much in class. [48]

He disrupted the class. The teacher talked to me about it. We went to the assessment centre ... Then they said he should go to a Special School. He went for a year but it was very hard. He learned problem behaviour in school. [He] just copied it. So I wouldn't let him go back there ... I thought: 'I've tried everything'. I kept him at home. I didn't know much about home ed. but I found out about it. [17]

The next parent withdrew her 15-year-old daughter, at the daughter's request, after a long-running battle with the school, which was dissatisfied with her attitude to school work. Even in the primary school there had been problems of a kind which indicated the school may have been holding her back. Whatever the case, there is no doubt that both parent and daughter had suffered a great deal over a prolonged period and that the daughter's education had inevitably suffered.

[My daughter] continuously complained that school work was unstimulating. This was all the way through. She wouldn't read the library books in the primary school. She said they were 'too little'. However, she readily read books at home and took great pleasure in writing stories.

In High School there was a steady drop off in attendance, and then only going to English and the Independent Research class. No amount of talk with the school helped ... They threatened to have her repeat classes, to keep her after school. They kept threatening to fail her. Then they said she's passed though she hadn't been attending or doing assignments.

[This meant] the school was satisfied. Their records were as they needed them to read. They said she must be very intelligent, in an attempt to justify passing her when she had not done the work. That was in Semester One, last year in Grade 9.

When she wouldn't get out of bed to attend school the counsellor said to rip the bedclothes off her.

I was approaching the school all the time, saying there is a problem and I want help. The message I got was that she was bad. She got the message she was not an OK student. They told her she just had to do what was required. Her response was: 'None of you are listening to me!'

She said 'I want an education, but not like this ... Can we try correspondence school?'

The correspondence school said yes, it was possible. He was sympathetic. He said he'd come across similar problems before. He said we'd have to get a release from the High School. [58]

School could also have an adverse effect on behaviour at home. A number of parents commented that their children's behaviour at home improved when they had not been in contact with school for some time.

I didn't like the way her personality was developing. She was picking on her little sister at home. She was quiet and subdued and lacked self-confidence and was negative about her capabilities. But it disappeared in the long school holidays. One year we took an extended three-month break from school in which she changed. I liked the change; she was much nicer. I didn't want to send her back ... So we tried an alternative school; they had staff difficulties. I said 'blow this' and then I went into home ed. [39]

Before he left school I got to a point where I almost hated him. By Friday he was so horrible I dreaded Saturday. I phoned my partner, who was working away from home, to tell him to come home or I'd kill [my son] – virtually every Saturday morning. [92]

[When he was taken out of school] ... the coughing stopped there and then. He had been cruel to his brother and that stopped too. They wouldn't be friends now if they were at school. [25]

The teachers said he was a lovely person. But he came home and expressed aggression, picked up from those around him, and then he let it out – it was not him. [1]

The following example is particularly interesting. It is quoted in more detail because it starts off describing what many parents would identify with, looking forward to having some free time when the children start school, much more so in this case because the children in question are twins.

The whole pre-five time I was thinking, I've just got to get through this and get them off to school. The first years were heavy going. I was looking forward to time on my own. We got them into Nursery for five mornings a week. They went in the Autumn term, even when they had whooping cough, because I was so desperate for a break. Nursery was sort of OK though getting them off in the morning was well nigh impossible, but I somehow managed ... From the day they started school they stopped doing abstract drawings. And they started wetting the bed for the first time since the age of 2. They wetted the bed very night during the first week of school. The twins had a class of 30 with two adults. I went some afternoons. I found it really stressful with the level of noise. When I came out I was really relieved. Do I expect my children to go here? We went through a term. They screamed when they came home. I often sat with them for half an hour while they cried and screamed. It was the same thing in the morning before going to school. After we took them out things cooled down. They did a whole year [in school]. I'd found out about EO at Christmas. Only then did I realize there was another option. I read everything I could lay my hands on. [83]

School could also affect children's general behaviour more seriously.

I had a huge job to get him to school. I thought it would get easier, but he protested every morning. I didn't appreciate how awful it was. They had been to Montessori nursery which they enjoyed. It was all open ended [after which] school was a shock – he became very withdrawn and slept badly. [79]

[She] spent most of the two years in the school suffering from depression and anxiety attacks and was put on antidepressants. I took her out of school in September '95 aged 13½. She had spent the first day back of her new term in such a panic she could take no more. The education system had failed her. [60]

She went to school without a smile and came home the same way. [30]

MAKING THE BREAK FROM SCHOOL

Official opposition to home education is well documented although recently there has been a tendency to much greater tolerance, guidance and even support, in both Australia and the UK. Similarly, in the United States, as Mayberry *et al.* (1995) point out, there has been a move from confrontation to co-operation.

The following families met with the more traditional professional opposition to their decision to withdraw their children from school.

The Head of the school seemed helpful at first but then he said 'No, you can't home educate'. I thought, at least by the time they catch up with me I'll have seen how it goes. [5]

When I told the school what I was going to do I experienced a Department of Education heavy to put pressure on me to send him to school. But we got on well. He was on a mission. The Head also objected. [25]

We had an interview with the deputy Head. His attitude was 'Look here my boy!' [90]

Most teachers we now see ignore us, except one who says what we're doing is the best thing for him. [My son] says 'hello' to the others but they ignore him ... The Guidance Officer used to phone us most days and say this was not the solution. [48]

When [he] came out I wanted to have his books. When I went to the school the teacher would not give them to me. She said 'Don't be so stupid'. She talked down to me. I then asked the Principal for them. He went and got his books. He was very unhappy about it: 'What are you going to do, teach him at home?' I made up a quick excuse and we left. Our main aim was to be polite as long as we got what we wanted. The Head said we'd have problems. I said I respected his opinion but we'd decided and he had to respect ours. The Principal told me not to take anything that belonged to the school ... [30]

Reactions could be mixed:

The school was not happy when we took him out. It was just that we were doing something different, showing some initiative. I felt he was being victimized. The fact that we took him out showed the Principal we wouldn't tolerate it. But the Education Dept was very helpful. We got a lot of advice from the District Supervisor, people to contact, including [the local home education network co-ordinator]. I couldn't get this from the school – they were very negative and wouldn't help in that aspect. [13]

The Principal of the school was very positive about my decision though he thought it was radical. He said that if I needed help or resources I would be very welcome. I don't feel comfortable about taking up that offer. A number of the teachers have been quite negative. [9]

Our dealings with the Education Dept were very frustrating – there was a lot of buck-passing ... We decided to go ahead regardless. Two people came from the Education Department, one of whom was favourable and one not. The latter was concerned that our approach to English Literature was not the school one of analysing responses to literature. Our approach was grammatical and critically analytic – pulling it apart. She was also worried about future employment prospects, but employers are mainly concerned if you can read and write. [55]

More recent changes in attitude were also evident:

Next year I told the Head. She was quite refreshing. She said 'If I had any children that's how I'd want to do it'. She was very positive. She said if there were any resources I need I could call in. If we did anything special she'd show it in assembly. [35]

We thought we'd better contact the Education Department; they were more encouraging than discouraging. [45]

When they were leaving school the Head said 'It's the best possible thing you can do for your children'. [79]

The local Headmaster is very sympathetic. [2]

My husband had an interview with the head. The school was very helpful. There were no problems. They even offered help, with apparatus, to go in at playtimes and to join in PE lessons. [93]

SUMMARY

Parents who opt to educate their children at home from the outset do not come anywhere near fitting the stereotype of the home educator: New Age traveller, hothouser, religious fundamentalist or crank. And there is hardly a mention of the 1970s doyens of deschooling – Illich and Reimer. What motivates these parents to educate their children at home, especially their concerns with the limitations of school, would strike a chord with most parents. Furthermore, there is no cogent counter-argument to the view expressed that education at home can be conceived of as a continuation of what parents have already been doing with their children during the first few years of life.

The reasons given for withdrawing children who are already in school are equally sensible and convincing: lack of individual attention, lack of work at an appropriate level whether undemanding or too advanced, failure to deal adequately with learning difficulties and bullying. More surprising, perhaps, is that some parents take their children out because they are disruptive in school. Whatever the reason for withdrawing their children, these parents made it clear they had lost confidence in the school's ability to resolve the difficulties their children were facing and that had they remained the problems would have been further exacerbated or at the very least continued unresolved.

In general, there was little criticism of school on moral grounds or for failing to embody family values. These did feature in family accounts of home education, but only after children had been educated at home for some time and parents came to perceive differences between children in school and their own, who were not subjected to either the institutional mores of school or the negative aspects of the peer culture (see Chapter 10).

Children educated at home from the outset settle relatively easily into home education. They have not experienced anything else. On the other hand, if you have suddenly decided to withdraw your child from school, the prospect of home education can be daunting, especially in the case of older children. According to one parent, 'It's suddenly Monday morning and what are you going to do?'

NOTE

1   Case numbers: 1–58, Australia; 59–100, UK.

Chapter 5

Teaching at Home

THE SCHOOL MODEL

We now come to the main task of the book, dealt with over the next five chapters, to describe and analyse how parents go about the task of educating their children at home.

Most parents followed what might be called the school model when they started out, teaching their children relatively formally, using 'formal' in the sense described in Chapter 1, i.e. preparing and teaching lessons within a structured framework, often with a timetable, giving regular written work and keeping detailed records. In other words, they did what most professional educators would expect them to do. However, only a small minority kept closely to this school model. Most moved away from it, in varying degrees, and just a few abandoned any structure whatsoever. The next four chapters reflect this movement away from structured and more formal approaches to teaching and learning.

Any attempt to classify all but the most extreme families would be fraught with difficulty. In any case, this was not a goal of the research. However, in order to give a very crude idea of the spread, 20 families, seven in the UK and 13 in Australia, could be described as relatively formal (of the Australian families, six were using Christian distance education packages). Seventeen families could be described as relatively informal, eight in Australia and nine in the UK. This left 63 families who aimed for a balance between the two.

The nearest that any home educating parents came to emulating formal schooling were those who used a Christian educational package, a highly prescriptive, very traditional and detailed step-by step correspondence course. A rationale for using such a programme was given by one of these parents.

> The ... programme guarantees your children miss nothing from a good basic education. Everything else you do as a family is a bonus. It's interesting to commit one's children to it. [He's] gone right through it. It's a great consolation to know it's a complete package and that he's mastered it ... From a father's point of view it reassures me he's been through a complete programme ... [8]

Apart from the few families who followed a Christian-based curriculum, all the other more formally inclined parents were faced with choosing their own books and materials, often showing a preference for older texts, acquired from second-hand shops, discarded by schools, or borrowed.

> At first we changed too many texts [i.e. kept replacing them], but less so now. We have found certain 'key books' for various subjects. These are usually older-style texts which had been considered obsolete by schools. To us they are gems, particularly regarding solidity of content, plenty of exercises and logical progressions. They are excellent for learning, teaching, drilling and revision. [26]

> Formal books work better; they both respond to formal texts rather than brightly coloured and illustrated ones. [76]

> We started off very rigorous because she might not be doing enough. We did maths, language, English and social studies. We followed the resources [borrowed] from the Teachers' Resources Centre. [14]

Human beings respond to the challenges that face them in innumerable ways. One parent, who withdrew her 8-year-old daughter from school because she had been failing across the board, decided to start from scratch, with encyclopedias as a basis for the curriculum. While it is undeniably easier to use texts into which a lot of thought has gone, there may be a certain satisfaction about creating your own curriculum, and probably more enthusiasm about communicating it to someone else.

> I started off with very simple reading books, to see what she could read and what she couldn't. With maths too, I started from 3 + 2 etc. . . . [Now] we do ten subjects, but not with a curriculum. I've got encyclopedias. I went though them ... drawing related things together, with page references to where each topic can be found ... e.g. dividing science into human biology, chemistry and physics. It took three months in the evenings to get this set up. Now we follow it. It's easier than just picking up anything. With history we started with the Stone Age. I've taken an 'as it happened' approach, not going into the Tudors or Middle Ages straight off. [98]

Relying on encyclopedias as a basis for the curriculum would horrify most professionals. But this parent had been doing so for nearly three years and had successfully undergone an official inspection. On the basis of her success she had decided not to send her younger son to school.

However, the concern of the research in this book is not with the curriculum but with the process of learning. And this is where the vast majority of home educators, even the most formal, start to move away from what one called 'schoolish approaches'.

INDIVIDUALIZED TEACHING

If there is a public stereotype of home education in action, it might be of a child sitting at a desk in front of a parent who is the teacher, who organizes a timetable, teaches lessons, explains what is to be learned, asks and answers questions, sets work and marks it, all during 'school' hours. It is an understandable stereotype because experience of school is all that most people have to go on. It is also what most professionals expect to see home educators doing. In keeping with this, when parents embark on home education, most start with the intention of doing school at home. They expect their children to produce a considerable amount of written work as evidence of progress, both for their own satisfaction and as evidence of learning for visiting education officials.

But even most of the more formal and structured parents found that home education turned out differently from what they had envisaged. Formal education at home does not turn out to be like school. Perhaps the most important change of all is that there are no 'ticks and crosses', as one parent put it, because misconceptions and other learning problems are dealt with as and when they arise. This is obviously because the parent is always at hand and aware of what is to be learned from the child's point of view. In consequence, learning at home becomes more of a continuous process rather than a series of tasks to be undertaken and later marked and graded as is more generally the case in school.

Learning at home is also more intensive, so that lessons generally become shorter and in consequence so does the teaching day. On the other hand, if a child becomes engrossed in some topic, it does not make sense to stop at a particular time. At home it is feasible to follow it through for the rest of the day or longer. This greater flexibility means that timetables are usually dispensed with quite quickly, although mornings are typically set aside for more structured learning. Another feature is that parents are often just one step ahead of their children, sometimes catching up on aspects of education they themselves missed out in school. Sometimes they learn alongside their children. Let us examine each of these aspects of home education in turn.

Learning at home is an interactive process

Children in school are forever being assessed. Work is accomplished with little direct help and then positively reinforced or otherwise with ticks and crosses. If there are lots of crosses, or whatever euphemisms for crosses are used instead, children may have to go on to the next step without being adequately prepared. The child's feelings of competence and self-worth inevitably suffer. Negative reinforcement, except when it is salutary, is rarely a spur to greater effort to learn. And if a child has got everything right it probably means the task was too easy in the first place. The only way of knowing if the material is at the appropriate level is when some material is understood and some is not. The whole point of learning is to move haltingly forward, making mistakes, correcting misconceptions, from a lower level of understanding or skill to a higher one.

In keeping with this it is well known that mistakes have a very useful diagnostic function. But they are optimally dealt with only if they are confronted as and when they crop up, a virtually impossible aspiration for a classroom teacher. At home, parents are always on hand when questions or difficulties arise and can spend as much time dealing with them as is necessary. In the classroom, children who receive feedback in the form of corrections, as they inevitably must, are interested more in how well they did, the grade or final comment, rather than in going over the corrections when they may not remember how they misconstrued or misunderstood what led to any errors in the first place.

At home, children are spared the frustrations consequent on an inability to understand or failure to produce acceptable pieces of work. Instead, they come to see learning as a continuous process. Obstacles to learning are dealt with there and then, or shelved until another time, without loss of face.

There are no ticks or crosses. I'm watching all the time. If there's a mistake I tell them straight away. If you mark it later they don't remember ... [He] had a lot of difficulty with basic writing. He wrote letters back to front. I've almost cured it by constantly drawing his attention to it. But it's got to be done straight away. [93]

... What's also beaut' is that, when teaching, you can't go on to the next step without mastering the first step. You know exactly what they know and what they don't. Whereas in a classroom situation this is more difficult to monitor. [26]

At school you can miss out a bit and then you are lost. Any problems can be dealt with there and then so they are over and done with. [3]

If [he] gets a problem when he's working I might spend an hour with him. [49]

Even in large families where learning was formally organized and highly structured, there was still enough individual attention to allow teaching to be interactive. One parent's approach had much in common with school except that the 'class' was much smaller. There were five children at home, including a baby. Each morning, the four older children sat around the kitchen table working from textbooks. The demands of the four as well as a baby meant that as much time was spent on managing learning, keeping the children on task, as in pedagogical interaction. Nevertheless, each child expected and got a considerable amount of individual attention. Here is a sample of her interaction with her 8-year-old son, in the context of attending to the other children, and the baby, and doing housework.

Mother: It's nearly lunchtime and you've hardly done anything.
[He is looking for his maths book – he finds it. They start to work together]
Mother: ... to find half a number, divide by 2. Half of 12 is 6.
Child: It's easy ... [moves on to the next problem dealing with thirds]
Mother: ... What can't you do? ... You can't just write '2'. You need a date, a page number and the number of the sum ...
[She helps him with thirds, using rods. He gets a 9 and places three 3-length rods alongside]
Mother: What about 18? If we know 3 goes 3 times into 9 and two 9s are 18 ... how many 3s in 18?
Child: 6.
Mother: Well done!
[He gets two 9-length rods and six 3-length rods]
Mother: If 6 times 3 is 18 then 3 times 6 is 18 ... Now, how many 3s in 12?
[He takes an 11-length rod out of the box]
Mother: We need 12 ... How are we going to find one third of 12?
Child: 2s.
Mother: How many 2s in 12? ... we are trying to find a number that goes 3 times into 12.
Child: Must be 4.
Mother: Hmm ... so the answer is ....
Child: 4.
Mother: Next is 27 – how can we make up 27?
Child: 2 times 10 add 7.
[He tries 7-length rods and places them alongside the 27]
Mother: 7 didn't work did it?
Child: Why can't 10? ... 8 doesn't work either. It can't be 9. [tries and gets it right] It is!! [82]

Altogether this session, only a very small part of which is described here, was spread over three-quarters of an hour with very many interruptions while the child's mother attended to the others, while he engaged his siblings in conversation or was waiting for his mother to help him. Nevertheless, his mother spent a total of 10 to 15 minutes, spread out over the session, attending to him. And nearly all her attention was pedagogically interactive, compared with school where individual attention is mostly 'factual and managerial' (Galton *et al.*, 1980).

In fact all the children immediately asked their mother or older sibling for assistance the moment they needed it, sometimes grumbling if they had to wait too long. This highlights the perception that home educated children have of learning, that there is no point in proceeding if you are stuck. This might be called the first principle of learning at home, that it is a dynamically interactive process.

Learning at home is intensive

In school, children spend only two-thirds of their time on task. It does not follow they are actively learning when they are on task, only that they are doing something which is interpreted as productive. How much of that time is actually spent actively learning is unknown. In addition, work is often not matched to the ability of the child (Bennett *et al.*, 1984). At home, on the other hand, children spend most of their time at the frontiers of their learning. Their parents are fully aware of what they already know and of the next step to be learned. Learning is therefore more demanding and intensive.

In home education you don't waste any time. You get on with it. [26]

I keep to terms but treat each term separately and organize it in negotiation with the children. It's what we're doing this week ... The terms are short. Last term was six weeks [compared with 13 weeks in school]. Part of this is because it is so intense. Lessons are the same, concentrated and short. [76]

Because it is so intensive, parents soon retreated from a whole day's teaching. A fairly typical pattern was to restrict more formal learning to the mornings, regardless of age.

I tend to have more formal mornings with 2+ hours of formal learning. I don't start at a particular time; there are chores to do first. [3]

We work from 9.30 to 1. We've got a structured morning because I've come out of the school system. [51]

From the start we had a couple of hours of work at least. Then it came to fixed times, from 10 to 12 and an hour in the afternoon. [5]

We generally work from 9 to 12 or longer. We tried a timetable but it didn't work. [6]

When we first started [home ed.] in February this year, we started at 9 to 9.20. Now we start at about 10. All work is done in the mornings and the afternoons are free. [29]

We started by getting into a formal routine, as in school. For the first three months we did a full school day ... Then we started with just mornings doing formal work and afternoons off. [10]

We felt he needed regular guidelines for security ... but coming out of [school] structure straight into nothing was not on. He wanted some structure and we've continued with it. [Her son, aged 14, continued ...]
Since I've been out I've done English and maths and some French and history and politics with my grandfather. I think he'd probably rather I was in school. He's a teacher [retired].

I spend about three hours, three days a week with him which may not seem much but it's one-to-one tuition which is better than one to 30 ... I go to him. I have a cup of tea. For maths he takes me through new things and we discuss them. For English, it's pretty much the same. We'd read it together and I'd do the questions. There are three one-hour lessons. It's boring sometimes but much more interesting than school. The first few history lessons were not interesting, but the one on the Civil War, the English one, was very interesting. [His mother added]
The rest of the time he does whatever he wants. [90]

Flexibility

Few formal home educators kept to a timetable. Most came to realize quite quickly that learning does not happen in quanta of 40 minutes or whatever and that timetables are necessary only in school. Lessons at home tend to last as long as they last, a few minutes, a couple of hours or, if a child's interest is really captured, for days or even longer.

At the start I thought all the areas of the curriculum need pursuing at the same time. Now it's done more in blocks ... If there's an art exhibition we take a week off to prepare for it. [8]

We do maths and English every day, at different times. If they get up tired there's no point. If we start late, we work late, though we usually finish at about 3.15. There are also mood swings. If they are high I calm them down with maths. [98]

Now he'll concentrate on an area of interest for far longer than he could in school, the Middle Ages for example. [51]

The children are all very different and they like doing different things. I try to develop what they are interested in to bring out their strong points. If there is a love of maths, let them go on with it. Once [one of my daughters] did maths for days in the afternoon – it went on for ages. [41]

[My son] became interested in chemistry. He'd do it all the time, but I gave them a spread e.g. another language and sketching ... [He] is going to Grade 11 next year to do science and maths. His main interests are physics and chemistry. He spent a year doing nothing but chemistry; he got interested in physics last year and spent a lot of time on that. [5]

An advantage of flexibility is the possibility it offers to adapt to the irregular and haphazard course which learning often takes.

At home – learning happens in spurts – one day is useless, another is very productive; that's why I'm anti-schedule. It is best not to do an hour of maths if you are not into it. [27]

Often I'd catch them just before going to bed; it was only partly wanting to stay up. They often wanted to learn in the evening. They were very receptive at that time. [61]

Shared learning

There is little shared learning in school, if only because most of what is taught is carefully prepared by the teacher beforehand. In fact, being on top of the material to be taught is a mark of good classroom teaching. But shared learning is an everyday feature of home education, especially as children grow older and move into areas their parents know little about or have forgotten from their own schooling. This would not do in the classroom, but at home it probably enhances the quality of learning because the children are active partners in learning rather than mainly passive recipients of knowledge. Furthermore, they gain confidence in their own learning, seeing that it is quite acceptable for an adult not to know. In fact, ignorance or lack of understanding simply acts as a spur to find out more. Again, learning at home becomes a process, this time a joint one, rather than a series of hurdles to be overcome.

If there is something we can't do we find out. [45]

Sometimes the parents get stumped. I say 'I haven't got a clue'. We look it up. It's a great educator for the parents. [26]

There's a lot of shared learning, of finding out together ... and I learn lots as well – sometimes we need to go to the library to find out things. [56]

A lot of learning is joint learning, for example algebra at the moment. I'm refreshing my memory as I go along; sometimes she'll get it first and sometimes I will. This tends to be across the board except, for example, if they are writing stories. [71]

We wanted to do long division. I'd forgotten how to do it, so we worked out together how to do it. [51]

You can answer their questions as they go along. When you learn together, what one can't figure out the other usually can. [34]

In maths it's backwards and forwards. If there's a problem we work through it together. That doesn't happen much ... if it's new usually ... We go through it. We sort it out together. [48]

We do a lot of shared learning. I'm having my own primary education. [25]

I only started to enjoy primary school maths learning with the children. I realized I had never understood basic principles before. [31]

I'm hopeless at maths. The other day [she] was working with shapes – it was great fun – I'd be learning too. [37]

In German I keep one step ahead. I'm learning with them and they know that. This also lets them into the learning process – they see what I have to do to learn ... In geography, history and science, we discuss how to find an answer and they learn from me as I learn. [10]

Here's a rather different example of a parent who had never considered home education but withdrew her 15-year-old daughter following a traumatic incident in school and was suddenly faced with preparing for entry into secondary college.

I had to teach myself before I could teach her. High School maths is not easy. I bought a video maths course. We cheated by looking at the answers first. I had to learn things like trigonometry and surds. [36]

The following is an example of shared learning. A child, aged 11, is working on algebraic fractions with his mother. It's an extremely shortened account of what happened over the course of at least an hour. They are both struggling to understand but there's no feeling of failure. There's a sense of knowing they will eventually work through it successfully.

Mother: Oh Jesus! ...
[She is having difficulty with addition of algebraic fractions; she eventually seems to manage and asks her son to explain it to her using numerical fractions. He writes $\frac{1}{2} + \frac{1}{3}$ and works out with her how the algebraic answer is arrived at. She goes off to the next room to work with her other child. He writes the algebraic solution. She returns to check, gives praise and goes to the other room again. He goes on to subtraction of algebraic fractions, then calls his mother for help and she comes back into the room]
Mother: It's the same system.
Child: No it isn't.
Mother: Yes it is ...
[She demonstrates and he seems to follow. They move on to multiplication. His mother has a go without success but inspires him to try again. She goes off again and he seems to work it out. No, he doesn't. He goes to fetch her]
M: Multiply top by top and bottom by bottom.
C: Does it always work?
M: I don't know.
C: Shall I try something to see.
M: Yes, multiply the denominators together – the bottoms.
C: What do you mean, multiply them together?
[They continue and check the answer arithmetically. Both still seem unsure]
M: [to me] I think he's had enough anyway. [She goes out of the room]
[He continues to work at multiplication and seems to understand. He goes in search of his mother who is now in the toilet]
C: [shouting and banging on the toilet door] I know how to do it! [76]

TWO DETAILED ACCOUNTS OF MORE FORMAL LEARNING

The first of these concerns two boys aged 9 and 7 who were taken out of school. Both their parents are teachers. It serves to highlight a lot of what has been described above. The way the family goes about home education is very much in line with what most people might expect it to be like. After the initial enthusiasm, the children start to resist a little and have to be brought into line. There's a timetable, a playtime and individual work in workbooks. The advantages of one-to-one attention are obvious and individual needs are catered for in a way not possible in the classroom. Another advantage is that it is much easier at home to go back to basics 'to get the foundations right' for a child who has fallen behind at school. It can be done without denting the child's self-esteem or confidence. It is more a question of starting from where you are at without implicit comparison with anyone else.

Their mother also becomes aware that the difference between home and school has more to it than simply being able to give each child individual attention. She notes, for example, that her children do not like writing, particularly about science, and comes to realize that the writing is not the essential part of it and so simply keeps it practical. In school, writing is essential because it is 'evidence' both of what the teacher has taught and of what the children have learned, or at least have filled their time doing. It is also an essential management tool because it keeps the class quietly and usefully employed. It is what parents and inspectors expect to see. At home, parents know what their children have and have not learned without written evidence.

With an eye to the next chapter, their mother is also coming to realize that a great deal happens outside the formal and structured sections of her programme, in cooking for example. The children also learn to tell the time by relating it to routine daily events.

They have greater opportunity, as well, to pick up things informally, for example, when they spend ages watching a worm in the garden.

I was filled with lots of trepidation to start with. I thought there would be two noisy boys around the house. But it didn't work out like that. They came out in February '94. [The younger one] was in his second term at school. [The older one] was in Year 3 and had done 2½ years in school and was nearly 8 ...

The first days were lovely. They were up at the crack of dawn. They were disappointed they couldn't start at 5 a.m. That soon wore off. After a few weeks of working willingly they started to try it on. We had to establish the ground rules. I had to make them sit at the table.

[Son remarks ...] We had excitement at the start, then it was a more normal way of life after the excitement had died away.

[Mother again ...] We still have little 'discussions' about work. [The elder one] would like to think he can get through life without writing.

I always keep to a timetable ... I was going to do half an hour English followed by a break, followed by number work. They were going to have a playtime and go outside. That didn't work. If they played for a quarter of an hour it was impossible; they'd be into a game or other activity. I soon changed. It's better to go on until the end of the morning.

After doing the basics for an hour in the morning they watch a schools TV programme. That's break enough. They work individually in workbooks in English and maths. I find it easier to put a pile of work on the table. They do a page in each workbook – spellings, handwriting, English skills, number practice and maths. That takes about an hour. I sit at the table or do ironing. Having two boys, they need help and someone to watch. If a question arises we sort it out. [My older son] had a lot of difficulty with basic writing. He wrote letters back to front. I've almost cured it by constantly drawing his attention to it. But it's got to be done straight away.

When we started I thought we'd do topic work in the afternoon. But [my elder son] is too tired in the afternoon to cope with writing. We do topic work from 11 to 12. The afternoon is for art, craft and physical activities, practical science, nature walks, me reading to them ...

I'm sure they've done a lot more than they would at school ...

After the morning 'break' we spend an hour on topic work, me showing them things or sitting at the table, writing and drawing. We've been doing boats this half term. Last half term we did the Greeks. Before that, the Romans, water, where we live, food – one every half term. In January we did 'all things new'. We've done 'space' ... The afternoon is meant to be about an hour. It varies. It doesn't just stop. It often tends to go on.

Science is practical. When I tried write-ups, they didn't like it. It didn't work.

Also we do music, singing, sounds and rhythm and recorder. [The younger one] is learning the chords on the guitar. There's piano, but I'm not pushing it overmuch. It's so easy to spoil the enjoyment. I'm a trained music teacher. My husband is a teacher. He was made redundant. He does supply [relief] work at the moment. Last term he was home a couple of days a week. The children appreciated it. He's a scientist, so he did the space topic with them.

For someone who's not a teacher, they feel they can't do it [but] you don't have to be a trained teacher.

Sometimes I think it would be better if I wasn't a teacher ... You get into the school mould. I know there are other ways of helping children to learn but I'd find it hard to break out of the mould.

They help with cooking, weighing ingredients, laying the table. They look forward to the time after supper, reading books and stories with Daddy. We learn a lot in the garden. The other day we went to an adventure park and spent ages watching a big worm, how it moved and burrowed.

It's better than school. There are so many advantages. It's good to see them enjoying what they do.

I took [my older son] back to the beginning and got the foundations right. We work slowly and his confidence grows with every new stage. He never finished work at school. He was classed as having special needs. He needed extra help but rarely got it. He now gets the extra attention he needs. The teacher didn't have the time. When he was in school I did a lot in the evening with him. But it's not the same as doing it in the day when he's bright and alert.

Now they both finish everything. There's no unfinished work. [The older one] couldn't do it on his own in school. Nothing was finished.

In school there was never enough apparatus for maths, but here I can find everything they need. And we use the natural things around. Learning to tell the time comes through the need to know the time during the day.

When [the older one] was at school he was emotionally uptight all the time. He hardly slept. Now he is much more relaxed and sleeps well.

The pace of life is much slower now, and calmer. I have time to train the boys in household things which we didn't have time for before, e.g. making their own bed, putting their pyjamas away. [93]

This next example is a very different one, of a girl aged 14, who was finally withdrawn from school after having been bullied since primary school and because she had learning difficulties. She was also taking antidepressant drugs. Neither of her parents had a post-school education. Her mother's repeated requests for an official assessment of educational needs had been turned down. At the time of the interview she had been out of school for nearly a year. Her mother's main concern was to give her a sense of security and a feeling that she could learn. She went about this by doing a gentler form of what her daughter would have done in school. Although her aim was as much therapeutic as pedagogical, she still came to realize that learning at home could arise from her daughter's interests as well as from what she wants to teach her. She also remarks on the pointlessness of continuing with something you do not understand. Her role as a constantly available educational mentor is also highlighted. Having her daughter at home enabled her to gain a much better insight into her strengths and weaknesses than when she was in school.

When we started home education we went very slowly to begin with, two lessons in the morning and one in the afternoon. I know you don't need to follow the National Curriculum, but she needs to get up at the same time as school and have the security of lessons. With maths, she was still adding on her fingers when she left school. She finds maths and English still her hardest subjects, but is improving more each week.

We work together as a team on most things. We go through the work together. If I think she can do it on her own I leave her to get on with her work in her own way, mostly project work.

She's much calmer now and she is slowly coming off her tablets. She hasn't suffered panic attacks since being at home.

With EO we go at our own pace. We get up at 8.30 to start at 9. We go through the lesson reading the book at first. She needs to go over it a few times, to make sure she understands, paragraph by paragraph. Then she can take it in a lot better.

The lessons are maths, English, music, drama, art, technology, science, PSE – [recently] drugs, smoking, exercise, green issues. In science we've just done volcanoes and earthquakes.

If I pick out something she doesn't understand we don't do it.

She chooses books from the library to do projects on. The material has to be of interest to her for her to take it in and enjoy it.

[She] has no basic foundations, e.g. in maths. The book she uses is such an easy one I can easily go through it. What I don't know I ask my elder daughter who has six O levels. If [she] gets upset and can't understand we go on to something different. I don't push [her]

when she doesn't understand as I find she will get upset and she doesn't take it in anyway
...

This year we've learned more about [her], her weaknesses and strengths. She's stronger than I thought she was. [60]

SUMMARY

The more structured teaching described in this chapter would probably meet with approval from most professional educators, though there are important differences in comparison with school. Learning at home is intensive, giving children more free time. It is flexible, allowing topics to be pursued for as long as necessary or dropped and picked up from time to time. With regard to the course of learning, it becomes a process rather than a series of tasks. Parents become guides rather than teachers, always on hand to help when needed. There is no feeling of 'can't'. Rather it is a question of 'Let's sort it out'. Consequently, there is little sense of failure or loss of self-worth. Shared learning allows children to see that an important part of knowledge consists of knowing how to find out, that knowledge is there, to be accessed when required.

Adapting to individual child needs, abilities and styles of learning, outweighs the advantages of professional training. This is not in any way to denigrate such training which is essential for the demanding task of managing the learning of 30 or so children at the same time.

Teachers could probably quote instances of some of the kinds of learning and teaching described in this chapter. The fundamental difference is that what teachers aspire to, but rarely achieve in the classroom, is a constant feature of education at home.

Chapter 6

Becoming Less Formal

ADOPTING LESS FORMAL APPROACHES

In the previous chapter we saw that more formal, structured teaching and learning, not far removed from what most children experience in school, take on different qualities at home. But it went further than adapting classroom methods to the home. Many of the more 'formal' families began to notice the part played by informal and incidental learning. In this chapter we turn our attention to the way in which almost all the families in the study found themselves drawn towards informal styles of teaching and learning, at least to some degree.

Learning in the early years is almost entirely informal, a great deal of it occurring through social conversation. Once children start school, the way in which they learn undergoes an abrupt and fundamental change. There is no scientific rationale underpinning this change. It is simply dictated by the fact that there is one teacher and 30 or so children. If learning in school is not properly organized, carefully structured and planned, the result is chaos. This is fair enough. But we have become so inured to structured teaching and learning, they are now assumed to have universal application, to be absolutely essential if children are to learn anything useful after reaching school age. Yet, while good classroom practice no doubt maximizes learning within the classroom, it does not follow that there may not be other equally or more efficient ways in which children can learn.

When they started out, most parents shared these universal assumptions about education. With experience, however, they found themselves drawn away from standard methods towards more informal teaching and learning of a kind which can rarely feature in the classroom. This takes courage. It means departing from the security of doing what most professional educators would approve of and moving into unknown territory. There are no handbooks or guidelines on informal, unstructured teaching and learning. Nevertheless, virtually all the parents, to a lesser or greater extent, found themselves moving towards less structure and greater informality. Some came to entertain the possibility that children might progress equally well without any formal input and just a few put this belief into practice.

Modifying structured learning

Although most parents ensure that academic material is covered in a manner they believe most schools would approve of, with experience they become aware of other ways of learning. Even one of the most committed 'formal' parents had relaxed a little. Her highly structured approach had undeniably served her well because her eldest son had won a scholarship, at the age of 14, to a prestigious private school. This mother spent each morning sitting around the kitchen table with the four children at home, working through textbooks. Yet even she had modified her approach a little:

> I've got less interested in academic very early learning as I've gone along ... [My 4-year-old] does not work, though she wants to because the older ones are doing it, and work for [the older ones] is becoming less structured ... a great deal happens in conversation. [82]

The next three parents described in some detail how they adapted school-type approaches.

> At the beginning we felt we needed to follow the school routine, and so did she. It seemed the only way. We used timetables ... We worked really hard at first, as they do in private schools ... but the privates are push, push, push. I'm not so keen on that ... After you've come out of school you just relax from the pressure ... We don't work as hard as at first. We are still timetabled. We generally do more academic work in the mornings ... We seldom do any formal work after 11 a.m. I tend to see the things she does as fun. She thinks it great fun to be able to decide to do things on the spur of the moment ... At school, learning is compartmentalised. At home she is learning all the time ... A few weeks ago we went to the supermarket and bought a cabbage. At 9 p.m. we found a caterpillar in it. She said: 'I'll write what happens.' It started to form a chrysalis, but it died – any old time for anything ... I like the spontaneity, going with whatever is happening at the time ... [80]

> The day is always reasonably flexible. I've almost always kept a timetable for the children, even before they could read ... I've generally had a programme as a guideline, something to fall back on, more of a programme for me than for them. The timetable is broad in scope, containing for example: jobs, music, Bible, tables, reading, creative writing, science, maths, handwriting. It usually covers the morning only. There is no rigid starting time. There is usually one major area after lunch. But if something is on the go, we'll forget the programme, e.g. [my younger son] is building a mouse house. It goes in phases, sometimes following the programme, then something different if something good is to hand. It's a blend of the natural, following the child's inclinations in a fairly unstructured way, and of the more formal timetable. [31]

> If it was a nice day we wouldn't start with anything formal – we'd go for a walk, come back, write a poem. I didn't want them to miss out on these sorts of things. There were bursts of interest. It seemed ridiculous not to follow them through. They'd catch up on the other stuff very quickly. It took a lot of courage ... when I still felt restricted by the government, like having to 'show' things for each day. Now ... it's not completely free. I admire those who are, but I would still be frightened. It would worry me they weren't covering enough work ... But they don't do formal work if they're on a real roll with something they're interested in. [3]

Loosening up some more

A remark which typifies the experience of many parents is: 'I used to try harder in the old days' [68]. Whatever it is about home education which shifts parents away from more formal structure, the pressure to change is certainly powerful. The following parents, who started fairly formally, felt impelled to loosen up, to listen to their own instincts, to try something different from school, though they seem unable to explain exactly what it is about less structured learning which they find attractive. They are just drawn to it.

> At first I was very strict and regimented with a timetable in the morning. I got all the necessary books but I later realized I was stifling the children. I've loosened up now. We've learnt that home education is not school at home. I've had to throw out so many schoolish approaches. They start with half an hour piano and then do some maths and English in the morning. The rest of the day is free. But I'm mingling with them all the time – following them up with whatever they are doing. [43]

> My formal teacher training gets in the way, but I have changed. I'm much less structured than when I started out. [99]

> Before, we felt we had to fill her with information. It's not the same anymore. It's a sort of absorption. Now I don't feel I have to know things ... [84]

> I tried very hard – things I'd like to achieve in a week – different methods. Discipline is a hard thing. Then I thought this year I've got to relax. She's got to get out of a school way of thinking and so have I. That was the hardest, turning away from expectations. The year was an experiment for me. I didn't make much use of school [type] resources. It didn't mix. I wasn't doing formal things. She'd been in school for three years; we'd tried the school system ... [35]

The only parents who moved in the other direction, towards greater formality, were those who were preparing for formal assessment of older children, usually in Grade 10 (Year 10), prior to entry into secondary colleges in Australia, or for GCSEs in the UK.

Trying to achieve a balance

Home educators often debate the balance between structure and informality and are aware of the range of approaches from informal, what some call 'natural' learning, to rigid formality. No doubt some parents were aware of this debate, but changes in direction toward informality were invariably the result of experience rather than ideology. This mother, a co-ordinator for a network of home educating families, in common with others who had similar networking roles, always advised new families to start off fairly traditionally, even though her own approach was informal.

> To most people I say to get hold of textbooks. I photocopy syllabus overviews for them. Lots want to do it but don't know what to do. They like the security. [57]

This is obviously sound advice, especially to parents who had never contemplated home education and had turned to it as a last resort. Starting out in this way provides a secure base within which to gain confidence and allows time to adapt to whatever approach will eventually best suit a given family and its circumstances.

Some parents who wanted to achieve a balance were unsure where to draw the line.

I'm a teacher. For years I've been looking for that balance between exploration and structure. They need to have different experiences and to observe the environment around them but at the same time they need some discipline. They do maths because they need the skills whether they will later use them or not. [41]

Children can learn a lot at home, not by having school at home but just by living at home – learning happens naturally [but] we have not been happy either with a complete timetable or with completely free time which we tried for a term ... hence we have developed the system we have now which is a balance of things that have to be done and completely free time. [63]

The overall approach is a mixture of structured and informal. [71]

We floundered a bit in the early years, not knowing what direction to go in and trying to get a balance between regimented and relaxed. [20]

I keep [formal work] minimal. It's one to one. He's quite ahead. I don't expect too much. I do all I can in the morning. In the afternoon we go to parks and on outings. I try to ensure we cover maths, writing and reading. They get involved in everything at home. They ask questions. In cooking there's weighing, adding and ingredients. At the moment they love kneading bread. You are learning when you go down the road as much as when you are at home learning. I won't worry if they are happy themselves ... There's no point in learning thousands of facts if he forgets them a year later. [86]

The following parent, perhaps because she was a professional school adviser, was one of those most torn between structure and informality.

A better way of looking at her education is to look at what she does naturally though now I'm trying to implement a little structure ... so that I won't be missing things out ... I feel she can't have total freedom. She needs the discipline of learning things in different ways ... There are expectations – that she must be seen to be doing something. I always feel I have to justify why she's doing something. I have to brush this away ... [24]

The main problem with informal approaches is demonstrating that learning has actually taken place. A school inspector faced with an empty exercise book, no timetable and no lesson plans, would be highly sceptical of a teacher who claimed that the children had learnt a great deal but that nothing had been planned and there was nothing written down. It takes courage to depart from the security of structure and written 'proof' of learning.

There are few if any visible icons such as a classroom teacher is expected to produce at the end of the day to demonstrate that learning has taken place. [64]

The following parents, whose children did not start school when their children reached the appropriate age, wanted, in their different ways, to make a formal start of the kind the children would have experienced in school, though with nothing approaching a full school day. The first found that it did not seem to make much difference if there was no organized input for a few days or even weeks. The second noted how informal learning could supplement structured teaching. Both she and the third point to learning occurring through informal conversation.

I try to organize things ... We tried $1\frac{1}{2}$ hours of craft, reading, maths and writing. If I miss a day it doesn't matter. Sometimes weeks go by without doing anything. [16]

[When she reached school age] she was ready to do more formal work and it suited her individual personality. Every morning we work for one to two hours on different activities. This made me relaxed because we had started. We've talked and read an awful lot, but real learning happens at night with story telling ... When watching TV programmes ... it's the talking that goes with them. The real learning goes with this, talking and dialogue while watching together, and with reading ... Formal learning interrupts real learning. But there is a certain satisfaction now and then from doing formal work. [11]

> She spends a lot of time in her imagination and we think that is good. However, we do insist she does some tasks involving numeracy and literacy ... The formal working sessions are about three times a week, up to morning tea. After morning tea they are banging their gums all the time. It helps them develop ideas. [23]

There is clearly a dilemma for 'middle of the road' parents who recognize the contribution of informal learning but who rationally argue that there is no surety that children will acquire essential basic knowledge and skills without a structured curriculum and some formal guidance and teaching. At least the school system is proven and professionally approved.

Age and previous experience of learning in school are obviously factors which need to be taken into account when deciding on how much structure there should be. The following parent took her son out of school when he was 13. She reasoned that having been used to school it would be better for him to be taught relatively formally. This was arranged with his grandfather, a retired teacher, though for only three one-hour sessions a week. She then decided not to send her much younger daughter to school when she reached school age. However, with her daughter she decided not to teach her in the same way, though still with some misgiving.

> With [my daughter] we've gone on doing exactly the same things as when she was younger. It will be better for her than for him, less structure, more of an evolution ... [but] it's hard to have courage to leave things alone and not to coerce. [90]

Letting go

So far, in this chapter, we have dealt with parents who tend to see informal learning in parallel with or as an adjunct to structured learning. The following parents entertained the possibility that informal learning of itself might be sufficient:

> They have schoolwork in the morning from 10 a.m. .... All this is more for my benefit than theirs. I need to know the basic things are being covered. I think they'd cover it anyway ... [28]

> I'll spend a few hours on a sheet and it'll end up in the jam. I get crabby. It proves the seamless [i.e. informal] way is far better. But when we do it at the table there's proof. But we are getting further away from that. [52]

So to those who abandoned structured teaching and learning more or less completely:

> My approach is informal and child-centred though I started off much more formally. [67]

> Sometimes I think we should do something but mostly things just happen ... she often goes to a friend's house and sometimes they just play all day, role play and games and make things, puppets and dolls and bead threading. I started off more formally doing work but gave it up because [she] began to find it boring ... I still think they should do something but mostly things just happen. [66]

One parent withdrew both her children from school, with the agreement of the headteacher, provided they brought work to show her at the end of each week.

> At first she said we should go in and show her work, and we did, but this quickly lapsed. I felt somehow it was for me to put on a performance for her ... I used to set things up for them and go to great lengths to explain to them, but not any more ... I now see us as carrying on living rather than me 'educating' them. [79]

One parent had educated her daughter at home, fairly formally. Family circumstances had then caused her to send her to school for a year. Then she withdrew her daughter again, but this time she decided not to continue in the same vein as previously.

> After a year in school [we] went back to a style of learning similar to that before starting school. [35]

Once children had experienced informal learning it could be difficult to reverse the trend. A parent who felt that her 9-year-old daughter ought to have at least some formal instruction, said:

> We're trying to maintain a routine of one hour on Monday and one hour on Tuesday, but we are lucky if we can manage that. [77]

There is little doubt that education at home becomes less structured, and not simply because there are fewer organizational and pedagogical constraints in comparison with school. It goes much further than the flexibility which even a formal approach to home education allows. Parents come to see there may be a genuine alternative to structured education of the kind experienced by children in school. Many are naturally cautious about informal learning. Yet they are still drawn to it.

HOW CHILDREN INFLUENCE THE SHIFT TOWARDS INFORMAL LEARNING

Most parents might not have departed greatly from the security of structured learning if they had not been influenced by their children. Probably, because it is one-to-one, they are acutely aware if their children lose interest and stop paying attention or, in some instances, resist anything that smacks of a 'lesson'. Because they are at home with someone familiar they are much more able to influence the way in which they are taught, though they are more explicit about how they do not want to learn than about how they do. As one parent describes it, they seem to have a vision of an alternative kind of learning without knowing what it is.

'Turning off'

One of the most powerful ways children at home have of influencing the pedagogy directed at them is to 'turn off' if they do not understand or lose interest. In the classroom, children are at least expected to give outward signs of attention or concentration, though this does not mean they are actually gaining any benefit from what they are listening to or doing. Feigning attention and concentration in the classroom have almost become art forms. But it is different at home. Parents are acutely aware when their children stop listening. There is simply no point in continuing. They remarked, variously, that they had:

'learned not to lecture'.
'[learned that] lecturing is useless'.
'learned to stop expanding on an answer when they stop listening'.
'[found] the feedback in one-to-one is instant and telling if a child has lost interest'.

In the classroom, children are not excused from a lesson if they are not listening or producing very little, in a written assignment for example. We accept this and tacitly acknowledge there is not much the teacher can do other than encourage, exhort, threaten a punishment or promise a reward, activities which take up much of a teacher's time. But at home it simply does not make sense to insist on teaching your children if they are not listening, or to go on and on asking for more effort if they are not responding. It is simply a waste of time.

At home, unlike school, if it reaches the point where there is little point in continuing, you can stop, do something else, even take the day off if you like. This makes sense if only because there can be nothing as unproductive as insisting on teaching someone who is not learning.

Resisting formal lessons

It is not that home educated children cannot adapt to the kind of teaching and learning found in school. Most do, when they eventually go to, or return to school. But many do resist it at home.

> It only works if you are excited. As soon as she sees a lesson in it she gets really bored. I back off too if there's no interest. [97]

> You can only thwart them if you force it. [22]

> I've learned they learn themselves. You can't teach them if they are not willing, or what is unnecessary. [57]

> Dad looks after [her] for me, one morning a week. Typically he says: 'Couldn't do anything with her today. She wasn't interested' or just the opposite on another day. [90]

> [He] does not function well under too much structure, though he's better now. He hated workbooks. I had to bribe him. [99]

> There was, and is, some resistance to lessons. [87]

Two parents, both teachers, were among those who recognized that optimal classroom and home pedagogies might be qualitatively different.

> [At home] we offer, but do not demand. [In school] I support more formal schooling and the National Curriculum because that's what works best in school. [65]

> She hates school work at home though it's accepted in a school context. [24]

Here are two more detailed examples of parents who had to cope with children who would not respond to school-type lessons.

> I had positive ideas about some kind of instruction. I wasn't going to leave him to play all day. For a while we had a time when he did work every morning for a while ... Then there was a big reaction against this, definitely. Then we stopped doing anything formal in an obvious way for nine months or a year. It used to lead to arguments and a charged atmosphere ... You worry that communication has broken down. [73]

> When [he] came out I tried structured work. I tried to get him to do a bit of work every day, but he was extremely reluctant to do anything. Sometimes I'd shout at him. He wrote

perhaps six sentences in all that year. He'd be made to do it at school. I was concerned if he went back he'd be too far behind ... [My other son] is just 7. I've relaxed a lot with him. I've given up getting him doing things [but] I did some work because I was worried about the inspector coming and having to show work he should have done. If you push him too far he becomes really angry. This is general. In the past, if he didn't understand and we were trying to show him, he'd switch off. I don't know how they'd get him to learn at school, but they would as they force children to become docile or biddable, but it would take something away from his character. [85]

In school, the only acceptable option on offer is to do as the teacher bids. The only forms of protest are minimal levels of compliance, passive avoidance or misbehaviour. At home, children do have the opportunity to resist more formal learning in a way their counterparts in school do not. Their parents soon learn that the strategies which teachers use to combat resistance are of little use. They adapt accordingly, usually moving away from more formal structure.

Children do want to learn

When children in school resist learning the obvious assumption is that, for whatever reason, they do not want to learn. Typical explanations include laziness, disadvantaged background, a poor attention span, 'learning difficulties' and so on. This may be unfair because children at home seem to spend most of their time in some useful activity aside from or instead of structured learning. They are motivated to learn anyway.

There's a bit of maths, English and spelling most mornings, but it always means I have to interrupt what she's doing, and she's always been able to occupy herself productively. [24]

Sometimes we haven't done anything for a week – so we must do this. But all their time is functional. If they don't listen they go away and do something else. [57]

I thought if they were ever bored I'd give them work to do. But they are never bored. They keep themselves occupied all the time. [33]

We are getting less structured because they do much more for themselves. Once you learn to trust them it's amazing what they can do ... [91]

[Girl aged 17] At school there is pressure to know everything that's taught; you learn it by writing it down. With Home Ed you know a lot without learning it. [39]

The following, recorded by a parent, is a practical example of how children go about shifting their education towards the greater informality they prefer. They seem intent on running their own informal apprenticeship.

After breakfast they [girl, 8, and boy, 6] raced upstairs and started playing a fantasy game based on horses, and I left them for a while before I gently reminded them that we had 'other things' to do (i.e. I wasn't going to let them play all day!). They said they didn't want to work with me, so I didn't press the point and went away to wash the kitchen floor. I was still out there when they appeared and announced that they were going to do some maths, but they did not want me. So they set each other some addition sums to do, all in different bright colours. Then they started on tables. [He] lost interest after the 2× table. Then [his sister] recited each one to me as I was on my knees in the kitchen. Then they drew pictures of horses and there was much conversation about these and about their imaginary horses. Somehow this led to [him] saying he wanted to construct a perpetual motion machine, involving a ball running down a 'very very very very very very long slope'. I pointed out that you couldn't have an infinitely long slope, so the motion wouldn't be perpetual. Then we discussed infinity, using mathematical examples including 0.3 and parallel lines and the beginning of a circle. [The 6-year-old] then got out a children's encyclopedia and read about perpetual motion, and we talked about friction ... [71]

One parent, a teacher, took the risk of leaving her children completely to their own devices when she withdrew them from school. The transition from school to informal learning at home was sudden, deliberate and complete:

> For the first few weeks after they came out [of school] it was awful. They just lolled around. I took them for long walks. After a month they started doing things for themselves, getting books out of the library. They became like sponges – couldn't get enough knowledge – about what they wanted to know and do. [61]

This is not idealistic. Nor does informal learning mean abandoning children to their own devices. The culture of the home has to be one which arouses intellectual curiosity and facilitates learning. Children need to have learning opportunities and materials available. Most of all they need a mentor at hand who sets the tone of activities and is there to interact and ask questions. What children are motivated to learn, from birth, is about the culture around them and how to survive, enjoy and prosper in it. Most of this cultural learning, especially in the early years, is mediated by parents. There is no reason why they cannot go on doing this, far beyond the age at which children start school.

Of course, if children are truly disadvantaged and have parents who largely ignore them and scant resources for learning in the home, then they will not learn much. At least, they might, but it will not be what the mainstream culture expects them to learn. But we are talking here about a small minority of very disadvantaged families or feckless parents, certainly not just those from lower socio-economic groups, who, as Tizard and Hughes (1984) found, rather to their surprise, were just as eager for their children to learn and to help them do so.

It is not so much that parents discover informal learning, though many do question the relevance of much of the school curriculum. It is more the case of children resisting formally structured teaching and learning, one of the consequences of which is that their parents gradually become aware of how much they can learn without it.

What are these children trying to tell us when they resist? They are saying in effect that the way they are being taught does not accord with their implicit and inarticulated theory of learning, an extended version of the one they put to such good use in infancy. The intriguing question, which follows on from this, is how far children can progress intellectually with little or no structured teaching, relying mainly on learning informally. We will address this in the next chapter.

TWO DETAILED STUDIES

There follow two very different accounts, both of which, in their different ways, deal with the shift from formal to informal learning. The first concerns a 14-year-old boy who was taken out of school when he was 11, as a last resort. The main reason was that he was being bullied. But he had also been a thorn in the side of his teachers from the earliest years because they could not get him to do more than a minimal amount of work. Both they and his mother were equally perplexed. He was apparently making normal progress with a minimum of effort. After his mother took him out his attitude to formal learning did not change one whit.

The four-and-a-half years since he was taken out of school make fascinating reading for anyone interested in a child's theory of learning. His criticisms of aspects of school-type learning are graphic and more convincing by dint of his age than those of forefront radical educational intellectuals. He provides an engaging and archetypal account of dogged resistance to classroom-style learning, gradually causing his mother to change completely her conventional views about teaching and learning.

Ever since he'd been at school the teachers had always asked us to explain why this normal child would not do the vast majority of the work they asked him to do and he was capable of doing. This was even in the first week of school. We couldn't explain it. There'd been no problem up till then. He was $4\frac{1}{2}$.

Every school and every teacher, that side of things remained the same. As he got older I was told that though they couldn't understand it, he was still learning.

At 8, the teacher had a set amount of work she expected of the children. She halved what she asked of [him] in the hope he'd co-operate more, but he cut that down still further. This never changed in three or four years, including teachers who took a lot of trouble with him and gave him lots of attention.

He progressed correctly. I've never had a comment he was behind. When he left he was above average.

He doesn't seem to like being taught.

He came out ... Panic ... Initially, I tried it like it was in school. It was the only way I knew.

We thought he was not co-operating with his work in school because he was ill at ease. Now that he was removed, he'd get on and work. But it didn't work like that. He behaved toward me in exactly the same way as he did to the teachers.

It did eventually get done on sufferance, with no end of rows and tears and exasperation on both our parts and a total lack of comprehension on my part. Why wouldn't he do anything? He was always alert and asking questions. But he wouldn't do formal academic work.

Because you are frightened, you don't know if you are doing the right thing. You've been brought up with doing X amount of work and neat projects.

This went on for two or three years. Only recently I've backed off. It's been a learning thing for me. I'm academically based and enjoy book work. It's the only way I know ...

For two or three years it was hell. I was constantly threatening school: 'If you are just going to gaze out of the window you might just as well do that in school.'

People said 'He can't go through life like that'. But I had a gut feeling going back to school would be wrong for him. I got as far as ringing the school for an appointment to go back, but I knew that was just for my benefit. When it came to it I knew I was instinctively doing the right thing by keeping him out.

But I'd given up work and he didn't meet us half-way. That was very hard to accept.

For two or three years he tried everything to get away from book work. I didn't know if the LEA [Local Education Authority] would turn up. I [also] felt I had to have something to show the rest of the family I was doing the right thing.

I borrowed school books to see what children his age were doing. I made sure I understood everything before getting him to do it. Then I'd get fed up with the battle and say 'Go your own way' and he would for two weeks and then I'd get guilty again, feeling I was letting him down if I let him get away with doing too little work.

It was so difficult when he wouldn't do anything. After battling all day I didn't want him as a son.

[My partner] didn't mind his coming out but he was very angry because [he] wasn't co-operating. He felt [he] was using us. We'd given him a lot and he wasn't playing fair. But he wouldn't do more if he was in school. I was getting more out of him because it was one to one.

[He] would sit and read fiction and non-fiction and do jigsaws for hours. He'd spend hours and hours working on his bike and riding it. He'd do gardening. He'd clean the house from top to bottom after I'd just asked him to do his own room. He's never been afraid of work.

He'd be very busy in his own little world, up in his room listening to music. Music is on while he's doing something else. He would rarely be lying on his bed.

By [age] 11½ to 12 the work gradually got whittled down. I couldn't keep up the pressure. It was too much for me. I asked him what he least wanted to do and we cut that out. We agreed we'd just do English and maths and science for GCSE and let the rest go – the other five or so subjects.

We did this for a while. I said 'I want you to be numerate, literate and have a knowledge of the world around'.

We started ploughing through Letts books. He was doing it more willingly. I could trust him to go to his room and he'd do it painfully slowly. He needn't have been slow. He was capable of working much faster.

I've found the Letts National Curriculum pleasantly set out and most useful. Going through the books gave me confidence but I was finding a lot of the work crushingly boring too, so how could I argue that he shouldn't?

But the more I did the more I asked: What's the point of this? Why write things down just to have them on a piece of paper? It's said you do this to revise, but it was pointless. If he'd been more malleable he'd have been forced. It was his strength that did it.

I got every book on education I could ... I was afraid if he didn't have GCSEs by 16 he'd be regarded as thick.

I now feel that what I did to try and force him was wrong. But it hasn't done him lasting damage, because he's strong-willed.

I still have to suppress my schooling. My conditioning is not to let him go the way he wants. But instinctively I know it's the right thing for him.

Now I'd say – leave the child alone for a year. Don't try and cultivate interests. I booked a tour round Westminster Abbey. The tour guide asked him: 'Are you interested in history?' 'No', he answered, 'My Mum is ... '

Now it's easier because he's older and he can go off and be independent without having me in the background.

Every Monday he goes to work with his Dad who has a gardening business. [My son] has his own mower. They go off early in the morning and come back in the night. It's all because he doesn't want to sit at a desk ...

I thought OK! No academic work, but I can't bear to have him following me about. For his sake and mine he must go out and do other things. I found out about conservation-type work. We said we'd give it a go. That was about six to eight months ago. It's all voluntary.

The first Sunday of every month he spends the morning at a Wildlife Trust Reserve, working on old cress beds. They also pollard willows, dredge and mow and do some picking up of litter, all under the warden. I didn't want to do it myself. They said they'd take [him]. He didn't want me to stay anyway. The others there were all adults and university students.

He wants to go. He's not forced. He looks forward to it. He can drop it at any time if he wants to.

On the third Sunday of the month he works for a voluntary organization at a wood [nearby]. It's the same sort of thing. He bikes to that.

Every Friday he works from 10 to 4 at the Cat Survival Trust. They want volunteers in the week and it's ideal for us. I phoned. They said 'Bring him'. We went around and they said they'd give him a go. He's been going for three to four months. He's the only child who works there. The Trust also looks after 40 or so feral cats. He does whatever they ask him.

He wanted to do these sort of things much earlier but he couldn't because he was a child. He does get a bit annoyed sometimes because he wants to do things they won't let him do. For example, they have a store at the back. He'd been thinking about how to organize the store. He'd say: 'I've been thinking ... You need to ....' He got their backs up. This was good in a way. I told him what he was suggesting was quite right, but there are different ways of going about doing it.

He's interested in horticulture as a career. He wants to offer a complete package, including garden design ... He'd have to learn lots of skills, some from his Dad. That's what he's saying. He wants to work. He doesn't want to do things he can't see the relevance of. He would do English GCSE to go on to a Horticultural Diploma if he needed it to get in. He'd do it because there'd be no other way.

Just recently I phoned the Agricultural College in [the next town]. I spoke to the tutor and explained the situation. I asked about books for an idea of what they covered in the NVQ which is more practical than BTEC ...

The tutor invited us to a Careers meeting. He said he'd talk with his colleagues. Under exceptional circumstances they will take children under 16, 14 at the earliest. The NVQ might be better for [him]. It's one day a week. Between now and then I can give him some assignments from BTEC, though it's more advanced. We can use the library. We went last week and got out some books ...

In the meantime we are putting a portfolio together, to show what he already knows and the work he's done. He knows the basis of building a patio, pollarding, soil testing. He's typed it up. It's basically to show them he can write and express himself. Also it's because when you talk to him he comes all over gauche. If whoever reads it sees [that he] can do things ...

I can only see our relationship getting better. For more than six months now I've stopped pushing. There's more time available to him. A lot with him is frustration. When he decides on his path he'll go for it. Till then, no one will push him. Some of what he does is to please me. I don't worry now. I feel I've done the right thing.

I'm grateful to him. You go to work for money. Now I've got time for things I've never done before. I've taken up interests from some of the things I've taught ... Not him!!

At present there's no academic work. He read *Lord of the Flies* and *Animal Farm* at 12. We discussed them afterwards. He gave me perfectly good answers, but if I said: 'Write it down' – nothing.

I gave him a comprehension test ... He'd ask: 'What for? I don't need to know about the leaning tower of Pisa.' I said what the idea of comprehension was. He said: 'You know I can do that.' I said that was what they expect in an exam, but that's not a good reason for doing it.

It's me who's imposed the pressure. I found it very hard to accept that what we do now is the best way. It's taken me four years to get here.

Before the bullying we'd never thought of home education. School is where you learn. I never thought I could teach him. Now I know you don't need to be an academic person to do it. He's thrown that in my face anyway. As long as you provide them with resources they do it.

It's being a resource and guiding rather than formal teaching. [88]

The second mother was drawn to home education from the start, especially after discovering, more or less by accident, the potential of informal learning. She still believes in a certain amount of formal learning but forever questions it as she sees how much her children learn through their own activities and interests, what she calls the 'natural' way. She has four children, two of whom are of school age – a daughter aged 12 and a son of 9.

This is the fifth year. [The 12-year-old] went to school up to Grade 2. Then we went to Europe for six months to brush up Dutch – the first visit for 30 years. When we came back there was no way she was going back to school. That six months opened my eyes to the fact that I could do it and they were happy ...

What made the travelling experience better was incidental learning, just living. Scotland was the best example ... castles and Mary, Queen of Scots in particular. She got totally involved in British history and hasn't eased up since – it all comes from that. This kind of learning would take place very naturally if allowed to. You can't pursue the interests of 25 at one time.

When they'd been home for about a year – no one asked us why they'd been taken out – I thought it would be an invitation for trouble not to do anything. I wrote to [the Education Department] to say we'd continued on from our trip to Europe. They asked if we could have a chat. We thought we wouldn't pretend for their benefit. We talked about the curriculum, continuity and work space. The guy was fantastic; he was really good. He said to [my partner] at the end, he said 'Hang in there! That's the way to go.' He stayed at lunch. He was very encouraging . . .

They have schoolwork in the morning from 10 a.m. Before that there is housework and morning chores, bringing in the wood etc.

It varies. [The 9-year-old] goes on longer than [his sister does]. Her only formal work is in maths – the rest is natural. Maths is irrelevant (I wish it were!). Maths does not come naturally for her, so we do it in a formal way, which isn't ideal, but a compromise.

He does more: basic maths, reading and writing skills. [My 5-year-old] is just learning to read and does half an hour in the morning . . .

I feel strongly about the way children learn, but I do the opposite every day . . . It's a bit frightening, daunting, experimental, to totally pursue incidental learning – so I feel I get compromised into formalizing the approach.

It's very hard to unthink everything you've been taught. I'm still drawn into buying textbooks. It settles my conscience. I automatically formalize what is natural. School is relatively new, historically.

I've decided not to keep a diary anymore – not just for showing someone [an official]. You are drawn into trying to make a good impression, using 'edu. speak' and exaggerating . . .

[She] cooks and sells cakes – works out expenses and profit and buys things with the profit. She'll get things from the Charity Shop and cut them for cloaks, costumes, etc. She's got into cross-stitching and patterns – fleur-de-lys – makes things in the way they used to be made. She learned how to make paper, about the development of painting. She's made seals with wax – medieval style.

It's not a history lesson. [Her] room is full of castle things. There are boxes she's made – with geometry thrown in. She's designed domes.

[He is] the same – he loves knights – he's made a chainmail costume – he checks with designs of the things he makes. He's also got into weapons and armour design. He's also into pirates and the [Spanish] Armada . . .

Topics fade away and crop up again on a different tangent. [He] is desperate right now to get to the library to find out about gunpowder. They are also into the Renaissance and what was happening everywhere else apart from Europe at the time . . . On Australia Day I was making damper. They said they were going to do a play. [The next-door neighbour] printed out the things they were: convicts, Governor Phillip, and they made a tape of bush sounds as a background . . .

My kids play and play and play and play – hence the conflict in my mind; on the other side is the 5× table . . .

Maths is not natural to me. I use books – a Primary Maths book. I select things, bits here and there, depending on their needs. [He] is well into maths. It's natural for him . . .

We go to see my father in hospital. She's now going to do a St John's first aid course. She gets a book out of the library on Florence Nightingale. She's read it all and summarized it and written a review of the book. She'll print this in her paper, as a serial. I'll be interested to see what happens next.

I can't see my kids going to High School. [Both the older ones] won't want to go. They actively would not choose to go to school now. [My younger daughter] might, I'm not sure. I don't know what her perceptions are . . .

Most of the children's learning is through conversation. A lot of my role is a minor role. The other day we were driving in the car when we saw a kookaburra. [He] said it was silly – if the wings were hinged further up the body he'd fly more efficiently. My role then is just to listen and add a dimension, that the bird would then need a different lifestyle. It's just being there.

He then asked how a hollow tree was formed. I didn't know, so we asked someone and found out. I'm tempted to formalize this into a project on birds. Then, I think you can't do this with everything. It's only some you do pick up like that. Conversation like this is particularly with [my son]. It's where so much learning is.

[He] writes a diary every morning. He has a problem with anything sequential. He wrote about yesterday and had problems with that.

One night a week is games night. We get fish and chips and play card and board games. [28]

SUMMARY

Most parents expect to have to 'do school' at home. This is generally reinforced by educational officials who want to ensure that home educated children receive an acceptable education equivalent to what they would get in school. The advice offered by home education network co-ordinators generally echoes this, counselling new families to start with school methods, plan schemes of work, use textbooks, and so on, at least until they have found their feet. Even those who keep fairly closely to this school model find it works out rather differently at home, mainly because learning at home is one-to-one, intensive, flexible and often shared.

Many families move towards more informal styles of learning. They begin to see that children can learn a great deal informally, without structure and without being deliberately taught. This is partly something they come to realize themselves as they appreciate the value of informal learning, if only as a supplement to more formal learning. It is also partly because children sometimes 'turn off' when they are being taught directly, in some cases going as far as to resist anything that smacks of a 'lesson'. As we have seen, the explanation is not one of lack of effort or laziness or lack of parental discipline. What these children are saying, in effect, is 'It's useless going on; I'm not learning'. Put another way, they are implicitly conveying to their parents that more formal methods of teaching and learning are not necessarily the most effective; in school maybe, but not at home.

Whatever the reason, most parents recognize the potential of informal learning and make some allowance for it. A few even abandon more formal and structured approaches altogether. This does not mean they abandon their children to their own devices. Far from it. It is even more important to be on hand and involved in informal learning.

Reducing the amount of formal learning, even abandoning it, does not seem to make much difference to intellectual progress. While there is no 'hard' evidence to support this, it is highly unlikely that parents will depart from tried and tested methods of learning unless they are reasonably confident of their children's continued progress. The disadvantage, of course, is that there is little tangible evidence of learning, to show a visiting official for example. Long-term outcomes of informal learning are also unknown. Understandably, most parents strike a balance.

Chapter 7

Informal Learning

As home educating parents gain in experience, they begin to realize that structured learning is not the only route to an education. A potent influence which brings about the change is that many children resist 'school-type' learning, sometimes strongly. As some parents respond by reducing more formal lessons, they see their children still seem to go on learning.

It is worth restating that formal and informal learning have different meanings at home compared with school. Formal learning at home would probably be regarded as rather informal in a school setting because it is child-centred and highly flexible. Informal learning at home is specific to home because little if anything is prescribed. Children learn through living, from everyday experiences, much as they did in infancy. This kind of learning is not feasible in school.

There can be few professional educators, or anyone else for that matter, who would expect much learning could accrue from simply living at home. There is no doubt, however, that school-age children who learn informally really do learn, which is intriguing at the very least. It challenges nearly every assumption about how children of school age should learn. For obvious reasons, very little is known about informal learning for children of school age – they are in school all day. We do not even know much about informal learning in early childhood. It is taken for granted. It is only relatively recently that research into language acquisition has demonstrated how language is learned almost entirely informally. Apart from this our knowledge of informal learning is quite scant.

A CONTINUATION FROM EARLY CHILDHOOD

The best support for the proposal that school-age children can go on learning as they did in infancy comes from those parents who, when their children reach school age, just go on doing what they are already doing. They have certain unstated goals obviously, to continue to develop their children's oracy, literacy, numeracy, scientific, geographical and historical understanding, general knowledge, emotional maturity, social competence and physical skills. But these goals do not have to be spelt out any more than they did when their children were younger. These parents are simply continuing their children's apprenticeship to the culture. There is no reason why learning should have to undergo a radical change at the age of 5 or so. Neither does the curriculum of the culture suddenly have to be compartmentalized into relatively autonomous components as it needs to be in school.

Children who start school have to abandon earlier approaches to learning that served them so well in infancy. But if they have the opportunity, as a few of these children did, they will go on learning in a similar vein. In fact, the idea of continuation was one of the reasons given for deciding to home educate in the first place (see Chapter 4).

> When he reached school age we just continued; nothing changed. [12]

> At the start it was just a continuation of what had gone before ... learning will take place anyway. I'm a trained teacher. [77]

> We felt there was nothing to lose. Why interrupt something that had been going on from before the age of 5? [89]

> We've gone on doing exactly the same things as when she was younger. It will be better for her than for [her older brother who was taken out of school at 13], less structure, more of an evolution. [90]

> I was doing a lot with [him]. He's really bright. He takes in any information. We always talked when we were out. I thought then, if only I could I'd keep it like this ... [86]

One parent who saw education as a continuation, still wanted at least to mark what would have been the first day of school. So, on the day, she and her daughter caught a bus and kept the ticket.

The lifestyle of these families attests to their reliance on informal learning, again being highly reminiscent of life in early childhood.

> Sometimes days go by without anything special happening. [71]

> There is very little that is organized ... We start the week doing lots of things and get to Sainsbury's by Friday. [70]

> Sometimes I think we should do something but mostly things just happen. [66]

> Children can learn a lot at home, not by having school at home but just by living at home – learning happens naturally. [63]

THE PARENT'S ROLE

Although children who learn informally have a large measure of control over what they learn, they are not going to learn much if left to their own devices, any more than they would have in early childhood. The parent is as indispensable for informal as for more formally organized teaching and learning. The child has to acquire knowledge about the culture from the parent who has to play an active role in transmitting or mediating it. How do 'informal' parents do this? Partly by cottoning on to what the child is interested in and extending it, and partly by suggesting things the child might be interested in and seeing if they are taken up.

Basically, I supply resources, tap into my wealth of information, see opportunity where it arises, listen and observe ... [1]

I'm with him all the time, as a guide. [32]

I follow them around. I try to be subtle and there when needed. Then they go on on their own. There is no entity of knowledge, just learning how to learn. [68]

Generally, they just did what they wanted, made things, working out money for other things and how much they would have to save. They'd watch TV, especially wildlife – that was their chief interest. Generally, I'd wait until they wanted to know something ... but I wouldn't then make them read or write about it. If they wanted to know about something they'd remember it – if not, if it came from me, it was far more likely to be forgotten. [61]

[It's] a question of offer and respond. If you have an idea of what might be of interest you make a suggestion and see how it goes; alternatively you cotton on to something that has caught the child's attention or is otherwise of interest ... [81]

We have antennae out all the time, sensitive to our children's needs, difficulties, interests, etc. [63]

CONVERSATIONAL LEARNING

If there is one aspect of the informal 'curriculum' which, above all others, contributes to learning, it is conversation. We have already seen how important dialogue is in more structured learning, allowing parents to strike while the iron's hot and deal with any problems immediately they arise. But informal conversation was also stressed by parents, whatever their approach. Again, this is an extension of the kind of learning that occurred in early childhood, exemplified by the work of Tizard and Hughes (1984), who demonstrated the opportunities there were for learning through everyday social interaction.

... lots of walks, we talk a lot. [61]

After morning tea they are banging their gums all the time. It helps them develop ideas. [34]

During a visit to [a nature reserve] he asked me: How do they harvest the reeds? We talked about the water table, end of summer harvest, drying out of land, etc. He didn't have to write about it; he had the answer immediately he wanted to know. It was a real life situation, no books, just human interaction. [63]

I always preferred going places and talking about things and giving them my attention, than sitting down with books. [85]

We talk and do things without too much organizing them. It just happens ... All the things you talk about ... It's incredible. [18]

Most of their education is talking to them. That's how I do most of it. If you answer questions truthfully and talk to them as adults ... Their questions are often at great depth. [33]

They share a lot in our talk – this is good except when you need time for yourselves. [37]

We talk an awful lot, from the time they get up till the time they go to bed ... It's constant, non-stop. [47]

We discuss things beyond his years. He's interested in politics. He picks up a lot of general knowledge from me because the two of us are in the house together most of the time. [48]

Lots of questions come up especially at meal times. We talk about people and relationships and difficult people, interaction with older children, being spiteful, being excluded, how to cope. Also moral questions, how you should try and be with different people; otherwise anything from ethics to astrophysics. [71]

We do talk a lot. He's a chatting child. When he was 3 we did a lot of talking too, I remember. [49]

They learn more from talking than with pen and paper. [50]

We talk together a lot on the long car journeys. You don't realize how much you learn. [61]

They learn a lot through everyday conversation and also learn to talk about their feelings. [67]

A lot of talking happens in the car. [78]

I'm convinced most happens through conversation ... I spend a great deal of time talking to her. [69]

A lot happens in talking, for example: 'Why don't we make this?' – or TV, for example: [a politician in the news] was 'stabbed in the back' – with metaphorical meaning. There is time to listen, and you can hold it till later. At home you can do a lot of talking and a lot of listening ... I talk to [her] about issues way above her head – this helps to give her a more mature outlook. I also listen to her – she might argue a point and be right. I did not see this in her school days – the relationship is not 'us and them' type of thing. [80]

[She learns] from being next to me, asking questions, watching ... What is important is me giving my time and not rushing off. We can take half an hour to walk down the street. [70]

In school there is obviously very little opportunity for learning through informal social conversation with an adult.

INFORMAL LEARNING NEED NOT BE SEQUENTIAL

In keeping with the above, some parents came to realize their children learned a great deal in apparently unrelated bits and pieces.

A lot of what happens might appear to a school teacher to be fleeting, inconsequential and muddled – but part of this is the opportunity there is to drop and pick up interests as and when you want. [71]

Children only learn if you are interested in the same thing. I have a prejudice against knowledge stuffing. Learning comes in a very higgledy-piggledy manner – we organize and reorganize as we go along. [74]

Teachers want things done sequentially. We don't learn to talk like that – not sequentially ... Some things we may spend five minutes on now and then pick up two months later ... I started with very little structure, but a sort of mental sense of what they should be doing. I had this big thick book. I wrote down what we did every day, for quite a while. I felt I had to prove I was good at what I was doing and I needed a record to show anyone. I found it really hard to keep a diary. We'd start on one subject and then go through a heap of things and end up 'somewhere'. They might read ten books in a day; we had tons of books. We went to the library book sales – books at 50 cents each ... For the school inspector I wrote down what we did in one hour: make a cake, do maths, flour, wheat, birds, flying, bird book, flight and feathers, timing the cake, heat, plan for evening, etc. [54]

If there is one body of knowledge the learning of which requires structure and sequence, it is maths. Nearly all parents, including the more informal ones, followed a maths course. Even so, the amount of maths that could be learned incidentally and informally, certainly at the primary level, attracted comment.

Organization is pretty open though I keep a maths course going, but more maths seems to happen outside maths. [71]

They do a lot of maths if [their father] is at home because it is almost a social thing around the kitchen table. [76]

We've used maths books, mainly to fill in the gaps with what they learn anyway, but lots of maths is with 'real things', practical rather than abstract ... Recently they built a cardboard castle with some friends. It involved building turrets, working out floor space, how to cut a spiral ... and no one mentioned the word 'maths'. [31]

A lot of maths occurs just through something cropping up ... maths just crops up. The children are always more ahead than you expect them to be. [75]

Maths just happens, though he was taught 'carrying'. [62]

This is not as surprising as it at first appears if you consider that most children informally pick up fundamental concepts in maths before starting school, and that a great deal of maths at the primary level is what adults use on a day-to-day basis, capable of being assimilated informally along with other common cultural knowledge. There are echoes here of the well-known study in which Brazilian children informally acquired mathematical skills through working in the local market (Carraher *et al.*, 1985).

Of course, informal learning does not just 'happen' without outside guidance. Parents have to seize opportunities to extend their children's knowledge as and when they arise. But opportunities do crop up very often in day-to-day living, even in maths. In cooking alone there is estimation, fractions, volume, weight, temperature and timing, not to mention biology, chemistry, health, environmental issues, etc. Then there is shopping (including price/weight comparisons), saving and spending pocket money, etc. In the car there is distance and speed and the relationship between them. These are just by way of example. It is essential for parents to involve their children in such activities. Even multiplication tables can be learned informally, just as learning the alphabet was, chanting them in the car, in bed, in the kitchen or out walking. Finally, parents need to react to their children's observations, answer their questions, follow up some of their interests, constantly extending and building on what they already know.

TRYING TO CAPTURE INFORMAL LEARNING

This is a difficult task because it has a great deal in common with early learning. It is so commonplace it can be almost impossible to pin down.

... [He] will be at a certain level and then leave it. He will then come back at a higher level without anything visible having happened. [22]

They pick up a lot just being around. I sometimes wonder, where do they get that from?
[2]

Trying to explain how their children learned informally could be quite a struggle.

It's not measurable because it's not recorded, but deep down I've always believed in children's natural intelligence ... We did about an hour [formal work] a week ... When I was relaxed I wouldn't force anything. [My younger son] is just 7. I've relaxed a lot with him. I've given up getting him doing things ... A lot of time I just leave him alone. [My partner] does a lot of practical stuff with him. I always felt he learned by conversation and by following his interests. He likes doing things in his mind. He leaves things if he doesn't understand them but he eventually does. [85]

What follows shows, at a detailed level, how children might acquire informally, often incidentally, what children at school learn formally. In this first example a 9-year-old boy develops an argument through logical questioning. He has just finished watching a schools' television programme on sampling, with his mother. The conversation turns to averages. It is an advanced instance of 'intellectual search' described by Tizard and Hughes (1984), who demonstrate how 3- to 4-year-old children might develop their cognitive understanding through persistent questioning.

Mother: Take four people in the room and divide by 4 [the ages are 3, 9, 36 and 54]. The average is around 26.
Child: If no one is that age, what's the point?
Mother: If we had a class of little ones ... If families have an average of 2.2 children then that information might be useful, for people selling things for example.
[Child keeps asking what's the point if no one is at the average]
Mother: If you know the average age – it's useful, e.g. at a meeting, if the average age is 13 then you know how to pitch it when you talk to them.
Child: But if you pitch it at 13 and no one is that age ...
Mother: But if you pitch it at 9 or 16 it won't be any good at all.
Child: But wouldn't it be better to have two groups?
Mother: Yes, but I can't [she runs a home education group]. So it is useful as a guide ... Now, piano! [62]

All children, whether or not they go to school, to some extent learn informally at home. Here is an example, observed by one parent, which nearly all families might identify with. It is just that there are many more opportunities for this kind of learning at home.

[My husband] came home [from work] and was standing talking to me in the kitchen. [My son] came into the kitchen with a book called *Air Battles: Air Combat in World War II* that he had recently borrowed from the library. He asked [his father] to read it with him but he didn't really want to just then. [My son] waited until there was a lull in the conversation and then started asking [him] questions about the cover. He wanted to draw a Spitfire from the front view and they discussed the perspective, what you would see from the front.
    Then they opened the book and discussed the pictures and the fighting techniques used. [My son] asked lots of questions. They talked about the Kamikaze pilots; although he had read the account he didn't realize that they actually took their own lives.
    [My husband] explained that they did it in the belief they would go to heaven if they died a glorious death. [My son] commented that he would rather have the fun of flying and enjoying his life on earth here while he had got it 'and then I can look forward to heaven later ...'
    [My husband] explained about aircraft 'ditching', looking at a picture of people being rescued from the sea ... then he was inspired to go away and draw a picture of a plane that had been ditched, showing the survivors being rescued. [71]

INCIDENTAL LEARNING

Incidental snatches of learning which occur in the course of everyday living are even more difficult to capture than more thematic examples of the kind described above. During a short car journey, spontaneous conversation recorded between a mother and her two children covered, among other things ...

> ... IRA bombs that [had] destroyed a flyover that we pass and some other buildings ... glass in factory windows not being flat because the reflections are distorted – that the glass needs to be floated on water when it is being made if it is to be flat ... making carbon dioxide which [the older one] did recently ... cranes lifting up concrete blocks and talk of balance of the weight at the back end of the horizontal arm of the crane ... talk of myths workshop to come and everybody wanting to be Midas in the role play ... discussion of savings in the Post Office, that you can draw out money at any one of them anywhere in the country ... there is a camel on a poster and it is related to a camel seen that morning in a book – there is a mistake in the number of humps on the one in the poster. What happens if you cross them? – one long hump apparently ... [68]

On another occasion, the same family had just returned from the park. In the few minutes after arriving home, topics discussed included:

> ... the sense of taste (sour, sweet, bitter, salt) which led to vitamin C and scurvy ... Tom Sawyer's cunning method of enlisting his friends' help to paint a fence; why he turned to face the wall when he was ill; how he was discovered when he disguised himself as a female ... chimney sweeps and how they had to be small ... this led to keeping underweight for jockeys and ballet dancers ... [68]

Here is an even more fleeting example in which a parent was writing a shopping list with her 9-year-old daughter. Her 6-year-old son came in:

Child (6): Mum, in an Asterix book there was a Goth called Metrix and he was quite fat
...
Sister (9): Did all the Gauls' names end in -ix?
Mother: Well, you've seen in Caesar's book, haven't you – Dumnorix and Vercingetorix and Orgetorix.
Sister (9): What does Getafix mean?
Mother: Well, um ... it's to do with drugs actually; you know some people take drugs, well, getting a fix is getting some drugs.
Sister (9): (instantly) Oh yes, Getafix is sort of drug-like because of all his potions. [71]

And from another parent ...

> ... in *Eighty Days* [he] had caught hold of the idea of 40 mph which brought in distances and changeover to kms, comparison with present-day travel. Then we were reading the last exciting pages of the book when Phileas Fogg had to travel 200 miles at 40 mph, and as quick as ... he worked out that this would take five hours ... [1]

In this next example a mother is cooking with her daughter. Some of what is learned arises from the nature of the activity of course but other topics arise as they might when any two people are engaged in an activity together. These were some of the topics they talked about.

- the nature of malt and how it is obtained from sprouted grains.
- the work of enzymes in the body, related to digestion.
- the effect of adrenalin on the body, especially in panic situations.

- the special properties of cats' eyes that enable them to see in poor light.
- eggs: she observed the chalaza in the albumen and wanted to know what its function was. She insisted on fishing it out of the beaten egg. I helped her to work out the purpose of the bubble at the end of the eggshell.
- she mentioned a book that featured a horse called Quest and said it was a strange name for a horse ... I told her about the traditions of medieval knights and their quests and then it made sense. [71]

Morsels such as these do not contribute to learning in any formal measurable sense within a carefully planned curriculum. It is more the very gradual and cumulative effect of endless, superficially inconsequential, unrelated snippets of learning which gradually fuse into a 'know how' of cultural knowledge. This kind of incidental learning was quite common even in the more formal sessions observed in which topics of conversation regularly cropped up which were unrelated to the task in hand.

An interesting feature of informal learning is that children are not faced with having to try to digest new knowledge which does not fit into or extend what they already know or does not arouse their curiosity or motivation. In more formal learning, children have to try to absorb what may not dovetail into and extend their existing knowledge in this way. Perhaps that is why, at home, they are more likely to resist more formal learning. In other words they essentially, if unconsciously, control what they learn, ceasing to attend when it becomes unprofitable to do so, that is, when they are simply not learning anything. Parents remarked on this, pointing out that when their children ask them questions they simply stop listening to the answers once they have the information they want or if they lose interest. There is no need to feign attention. The realization that once children turn off, there is no point in continuing, led some parents to be willing to let go and not insist on seeing every teaching opportunity through to the end. For example, a child (aged 6) was counting two piles of cherries she had just picked.

Mother: How many altogether?
Child: I can't count them.
Mother: How do you count them so you don't get muddled up?
Child: Mmmm ... 22
Mother: 11 and 9 don't make 22. Count them again ... [72]

She did not pursue this, just let her daughter know she had gone wrong somewhere. In another instance a mother used the word 'intricate' to describe a mosaic pattern. Her son asked 'What's intricate?' but had already turned to something else before his mother had time to complete her explanation. She did not persist or demand his attention. He had made a meta-cognitive decision that his attention was more usefully directed elsewhere. Perhaps his decision was wrong and a learning opportunity lost. But his mother knows, from experience, that if she insists on having his attention it is likely to be feigned or half-hearted. The converse of this is that parents can really capitalize when children do 'switch on' their attention. They are much more likely to be in the 'zone of proximal development' and therefore profit from attending. That is also why parents, especially those who use more informal methods, have constantly to 'keep their antennae out', as one described it.

There are two aspects of conversation in informal learning which are particularly enriching. The first is that much of it is spontaneous and social in which the child is an equal and active partner and almost certainly unaware that s/he is 'learning'. As one 17-year-old girl mused: 'With Home Ed you know a lot without learning it' [39].

Second, the conversation is with an adult who, relatively speaking, has expert knowledge of the culture, offering what Rogoff (1990) terms 'guided participation'. Of course, all children learn in this way to some extent when they are at home. It would be interesting to find out just how much of what is achieved at school, certainly primary school, might actually be ascribed to incidental learning outside school, mainly at home. There is some support for this from a study called *Summer Learning* in which children from advantaged homes were found to progress intellectually at the same rate during the long (10-week) American summer vacation (when they were supposedly taking a long-awaited break from 'learning') as they did at school. In deference to school it needs to be added that the finding did not apply to children from disadvantaged homes, who regressed during the vacation (Heyns, 1978).

There is nothing new about informal learning. What is new is the prospect that such learning, of itself, might be sufficient for a rate of intellectual development at least equal to that of school, through and beyond the primary level, without carefully planned professional input for five hours a day in the classroom, plus homework.

INFORMAL LEARNING CAN BE SUSTAINED AS WELL

As children grow older they become capable of more sustained learning, especially after they have learned to read and can therefore acquire knowledge independently. Learning is still informal in that it is not planned beforehand, but projects and topics can be pursued for days, weeks or longer. Children can follow through on anything that captures their interest, with an encouraging mentor on hand to share in the learning, be a sounding board, guide, answer questions and provide feedback.

If there is any direct teaching done by parents who rely on informal learning, it is teaching their children how to learn rather than what to learn, to concentrate for long periods of time and to develop research skills.

> What I taught her was research skills. That's all you need to find out about any subject. We'd go to the library and just pick out books she was interested in. Once she asked me about government. We went into the whole Westminster system, back to Cromwell. [54]

> Sometimes she gets a new lease of life or a new idea e.g. at 10 p.m., so, out come the books because she's switched on; you have to tap into that. Also when they show an interest you can flog it; when this happens they will go on and on and on, hardly stopping for a meal. [61]

> [She] will concentrate for long periods if she wants to master something. [70]

> We've taught them from the start to concentrate on things for a long time. They'll start a project and keep it going all day. [One of them] decided she was going to grind wheat to make flour. In the end she gave up, but she'd kept at it for ages. [33]

> A curriculum doesn't matter ... I don't plan much. I let them lead. One night we looked at the stars and it went on and on. He's writing to a friend about it. He's learned about constellations and he's looking out for Jupiter and Venus each night. [12]

> Topics tend to crop up because they are sparked off by something, for example, they went to an event in which they dressed up as Tudor peasants and this led to a project on the Stuarts which lasted for months. [71]

Sometimes children can become genuine experts in fields or topics which have enthused them. One child did nothing but chemistry for a year. He eventually went on to outstanding achievement in the subject at a national level, both before going to school and subsequently in school. Another became fascinated with politics in general and the Russian Revolution in particular. On going to school for the final year she was astonished at the lack of knowledge of the subject on the part of her specialist history teacher who was covering the topic specifically for a university entrance examination. These are just two of many examples.

TWO INFORMAL APPROACHES IN MORE DETAIL

The first family consists of three children of school age plus three younger ones. The eldest girl, taken out of school at 8 years of age, resisted more formal teaching at home, with an 'ugh!' attitude to school-type lessons. But, as her mother says, she knows what she does not want more clearly than what she does. She seems to have a different vision of learning without knowing what it is. She is not lazy. When her mother relaxes her more structured regime, her daughter does not cease to be productively occupied. She simply does not waste energy on what she does not want to do, but it does not mean she is selfishly learning a narrow range of material relevant to her only. She is way ahead of school requirements when she goes to school for a period towards the end of the school year. Moreover, in common with other home educated children, she adapts readily to classroom learning when she does go to school. It is just that she does not tolerate it at home. There is no doubt that she covers a great deal of ground at home. Her mother is flabbergasted when she keeps a journal at just how broad her daughter's interests are. She comes to realize there is no need for learning at home to be structured, either for this daughter or for the others, though there does need to be a considerable amount of interaction with herself. Like nearly everyone else though, she still needs the security of at least a certain amount of formal learning.

> When we started I thought we ought to sit down and do school with a blackboard. We talked about trade and how it affects different people, from the primary producer to the ship. She [the eldest] tried to be the little schoolgirl, but she had a different vision but didn't know what it was. We persisted for two weeks, then it slacked off ...
>
> After a month or two [of being like school] we burned out. The pressure got beyond a joke. She said 'You're my mother, not my teacher'. She wanted one-to-one. She wanted help right at the moment she needed it. Although she didn't like the general approach anyway, she was still very demanding. She burned me out. She was virtually impossible to teach in a formal environment. I always had to be there with her to get her to do anything. She complained constantly and bitterly. It was very difficult with the other four or five children needing attention.
>
> So we just went out and did lots of things. I kept a journal of all the learning things. At the end of six months I drew up a chart in readiness for the next visit. I was flabbergasted at the amount of learning taking place, for example through discussion, experience, being out and about. The feedback was phenomenal.
>
> They don't run wild but have meaningful things to do, lots of problem solving and planning. For a while I made up work sheets with problem-solving riddles, etc., incorporating various kinds of learning material. They enjoyed it to a degree. But that was a lot of work.
>
> During the first six months [she] refused point blank to do creative writing and rebelling against school work became a huge issue. It lasted into the next year.
>
> I was frank [with the District Officers]. I showed them what I tried to do was to get ideas to germinate, e.g. using a story tape to get them to write. I tried five or six different methods

with her for creative writing, but at the end of the day, it was up to her to want to do it, and the District Officers agreed that I had done as much if not more than the average school teacher in trying to encourage her ...

Then we went to a museum. The next day she wrote out a story and over three days we edited it – it took five drafts. I showed it to a friend, who said 'She can write stuff when she needs to, better than some in High School'. She was Grade 5 [aged 10] at the time.

This kind of learning was an ongoing thing with her. She didn't read until late in Grade 1, in her own time. She doesn't waste energy on what she doesn't want to do. She whinges.

Lots of issues came up that made me put them back in school for six weeks. Towards the end of the second year I'd done very little academic work over the previous six months. They went to school for the last six weeks of the year. [She, the eldest] was head and shoulders above the rest, in the top 10 per cent in everything – at the end of Grade 6.

I was flabbergasted. During the previous six months she'd either learned nothing, or she had learned a lot in that time. [My second daughter who had never been in school] was one or two grades above her age. [The third child] was an average pre-schooler, happy to be in a group doing fun things.

They've learned to keep themselves busy.

I just trust things will happen in their own sweet time. I like social studies and science. I'll create a situation where they may be interested, but I won't go out of my way to make it sink in. If they don't take any interest I'll leave it. Sometimes, later on, they'll come back to it.

Once we were walking down a street with high modern buildings. [My eldest] said they were lovely and I said 'Yuk!' Then we went down a street where there were very old houses. She said how different the feeling was. The atmosphere was completely different; you can smell it's been around for years. We talked about it. With the conversation we were having about it she appreciated the difference. If she'd been in a schoolroom it couldn't have happened like that.

It was in incidental things like that, being there, feeling it. You can read it in a book, but to walk down the street and realize there would have been trams and horses and carts there ...

If my children do structured work it's two hours in the morning and that's it. The rest is being busy, creative, or just doing nothing, or going out.

I didn't achieve what I intended to but she did lots of things she wouldn't have done in school. This is from an academic perspective. I can't get the spark into her for being keen on learning. In that respect I felt I hadn't achieved much. She always has an 'ugh!' attitude whenever I suggested school work.

But she's very self-confident and good at understanding things which are relevant for her. She's objective, not relying on what she's told. She wouldn't do anything until it clicked, until she understood. Then she'd go ahead. As soon as there was any pressure she'd just rebel. It was definitely not the experience I was hoping for but it was a new perspective for her.

From a philosophical perspective school is not necessary. I know they can learn as well if not better outside. Even if we do drop off for six months, one day we'll go into binge mode and they'll streak ahead.

For the children it's relaxed. In the morning I try to get them to do something, play a game or do a puzzle. A game might be very intensive, with role play, exploring relationships, etc. But there's little TV and no messing around, no non-productive stuff. So long as they're thinking, creative, etc. it's OK. I'm happy to sit back if they're involved. Sometimes what they do is very complex.

The fundamental thing I'm pursuing is giving them a childhood. It's exploring. They watch everything going on. There's a freedom to pursue their interests.

You don't need to be trained [to home educate]. You only need to be interested, motivated.

So, there are lots of things in which they get involved and some in which they don't.

There must be some outside interaction for them to learn. There must be a sharing aspect. But it doesn't have to be structured. It happens informally. [57]

The second example concerns a girl who was taken out of school at the age of 11 and educated informally at home until she was 16, when she returned to the final year of secondary college prior to going to university. At the time of the interview she was 17. She was one of only two children in the study to be educated informally up to this level (Grade 11/GCSE). She, too, found no difficulty with school when she returned after a five-and-a-half-year gap.

Both mother and daughter participated in the interview.

Mother: [There were] difficulties with school; [she] came out half-way through Grade 6 (six years ago). She has now been back in school for half a year.

She was going through the state system. I didn't like the way her personality was developing. She was picking on her little sister at home. She was quiet and subdued and lacked self confidence and was negative about her capabilities. But it disappeared in the long school holidays.

One year we took an extended three-month break from school in which she changed. I liked the change; she was much nicer. I didn't want to send her back. So we tried an alternative school; they had staff difficulties. I said 'blow this' and then I went into Home Ed. I sort of knew about it but didn't know anyone doing it. I had read John Holt though. I thought 'Hang on! Why not?' She was then 11.

Daughter: I was really relieved. I didn't want to go back to school. I just hated it generally.

Mother: There was no problem with school work. All the teachers kept on telling me what a lovely student she was. Academically, she was doing fine. It was just a relief when she came out.

I started frequenting book shops and some shops with books for school. I hunted around. [She] spent a lot of time in the Bush; it was very informal. I had taught in High School – this was useful as a guide. I had nothing particular in mind. I'd taught long enough in school to realize that what you learned in school was not retained beyond the last exam. And facts are not important.

There was no structured work ...

Daughter: It just happened; there were educational programmes on TV.

Mother: I read heaps; we made attempts to sit down and do things and they led to other things. When I think back things did happen but I didn't think of planning them. I have to plan now because there are four [much younger children between 5 and 11].

It was very informal with her up to Grade 10 – there was very little structure. Then we panicked in Grade 10. People tell you about what you need to do to get jobs. I got worried, but we didn't do much more. We'd work really hard for a few days, then it would be informal again. We couldn't keep up the formal work. We still can't ...

Everything else just happened – all this was illegal. I'm now legal and I've been told I should keep records – including what they do. But I've not kept records; it's the doing that matters.

Daughter: I was really into politics for a few years, off and on, sometimes intensive. I got interested in communism, fascism, Australian government, etc. I'd heard of communism as an insult. It wasn't really like that. I got interested when there was an election on. I knew a lot about the Russian Revolution. We are doing it [now] at school. It's boring and sometimes the teacher gets it wrong and it's embarrassing. I pointed out a few things and the teacher said 'OK'.

Mother: [She] stayed at home for Grade 11. She was going to go to [Secondary] College but she didn't have Grade 10 marks. So she stayed at home. It took a lot of messing around to find out what was needed [for Grade 11]. The whole process went on and on; I had to keep ringing up, etc. It was very frustrating ...

It was half-way through Grade 11 before we got the texts. We had to get a Course statement. The information provided was poor. Then she went on with her own devices. We talked a lot – to all hours, sometimes into the morning.

Daughter: I don't know what I know about anything till I've talked with someone, e.g. to find out deeper meanings and to see how it affects society.
Mother: She started school in Grade 12, doing Humanities.
Daughter: I'll go to Uni. next year. I want to work in writing or in film – anything to do with film.

School is very 'schooly', frustrating, so much time waiting for things to happen, waiting for someone to come, not having the right copy of things, waiting round while the teacher is helping others.

But I like school. I love the subjects I'm doing. I like interaction with teachers and other students. I like going out to the library – you can come and go. I thought I'd be very behind. How was I going to cope with so many subjects? But it's been really easy.
Mother: I felt she could cope but I was surprised at how well she did ...
Daughter: At school there is pressure to know everything that's taught; you learn it by writing it down. With Home Ed you know a lot without learning it.

Other kids were jealous that I was at home. They gave me long lectures. Some would say 'I go, so you should ... '.
Mother: It [informal education] wasn't confidence. I couldn't think of anything else to do at the time. [39]

There is one essential element missing from the description and analysis of informal learning in this chapter – evidence of actual increments in learning. There have been claims for informal and incidental learning. Many opportunities and conversations in which children might learn informally have been described. But we have not seen a child actually moving from a lower level of conceptualization or skill to a higher one through informal learning. It is to this we turn in the next chapter.

SUMMARY

Informal learning has much in common with learning in infancy. A great deal of it occurs through what appears on the surface to be everyday social conversation, but which on closer analysis contains many opportunities for learning. It does not need to be sequential, not even in maths. It is as if the children themselves impose their own sequence. Although much informal learning is incidental, it does not mean that it is all piecemeal. If children develop a particular interest in a topic, they may pursue it at length, for weeks or months.

Again, as with early learning, the role of the parent as guide and mentor is crucial, though as children grow older they obviously become more capable of learning independently, especially after becoming literate.

Chapter 8

A Chronicle of Informal Learning

Over the last three chapters we have looked at highly structured to completely informal styles of teaching and learning. Professional educators might acknowledge, some grudgingly perhaps, that children can be taught effectively at home by unqualified parents provided they keep to the kind of learning their children would have experienced in school. However, the notion that effective education can proceed informally, simply through the course of everyday living, even into the secondary years, is another matter. It directly confronts and challenges nearly two centuries of received wisdom derived from the study of teaching and learning in school.

In the previous chapter we saw how parents described experiences which might have contributed to learning informally. But we have not actually 'seen' real increments in learning by informal means, that is, progressing from one level of knowledge to a higher one without systematic and deliberate teaching.

The main purpose of this chapter is to actually chronicle informal learning as it happens. This would not have been feasible if one of the parents, whose approach was informal, had not become engrossed in her daughter's learning. She started out with the intention of recording just a few instances of learning in keeping with part of the initial intentions of the research. In the event she kept a very detailed journal of learning and other home educating experiences from when her daughter was just 7 years old. It was not until I started to go over the journal that the possibility of a chapter of this nature was conceived.

The sheer difficulty of recording instances of learning or experiences which might contribute to learning was brought home to me when I spent some time with the family. Something I had not even noticed would be written down in the journal. Normally, it is only milestones in development which capture parental attention – the first step or the first word. The fact that children are learning all the time through routine, everyday living, goes unnoticed.

Space does not permit doing justice to the richness and variety of learning described in this one parent's journal. For the purpose of this exercise I have restricted myself to mathematics, and only to one aspect in detail, the child's developing understanding of money. Maths was chosen because increments in understanding are much clearer and progress therefore much easier to observe.

Let us call the child Alice.

Alice's progress in maths is not intended to be compared with age-related norms. The intention is only to describe the process of informal learning, to demonstrate that a child actually can learn mathematics, certainly at the primary level, through informal, unstructured, mostly incidental learning.

Alice's mother was not ideologically committed to her daughter learning maths informally. From time to time she frankly questions much of what she is doing, how much formal maths she should do, even whether she really wants to be home educating at all! During the course of the journal she often raises doubts about the untried aspects of informal learning, for example:

> Last night I was feeling that Alice's home ed. is leading nowhere. Thinking back over the diaries I feel like we just seem to have a whole heap of false starts which we fail to follow up, a bag of bits and pieces which aren't forming anything concrete.

As she reasons, her daughter has only got one chance at an education and at least the formal method of learning maths is a proven one. On just one or two occasions she resorts to more structured learning in maths, but they always peter out after a week or so. More regularly she tries to get Alice to learn her tables, with little success.

An important feature of learning maths informally is that it is usually impossible to divorce it from the activity in which it is embedded. For example, on one occasion, Alice is buying a piece of fruit to eat. Her choice depends partly on price. This is not about 'If one orange costs 50 cents how many can I buy with $3?', which is hardly different from 'How many 50¢ in $3?' when it is out of context, as it has to be in the classroom. For Alice, the activity is buying real fruit, to eat there and then, not maths. Similarly, when cooking, her mother uses the opportunity to introduce measurement of weight and time, fractions and geometry (shapes of bread). But this is part and parcel of acquisition of more general cultural knowledge to do with cooking, not about maths isolated from other activities. For Alice the activity is baking bread or cakes.

A disadvantage of informal learning of this kind, as we shall see, is that Alice finds it quite difficult, for some reason, to transfer her practical understanding of maths to out-of-context situations. This became very obvious to me when, during a visit, I played a game of Number Lotto with her. She found difficulty with the easiest of calculations. But the next minute she was able to display a far higher level of understanding in relation to calculation of time and money, both of which had immediate practical relevance for her. This also applied to learning her tables which for her was a painfully slow process. However, when she had not even fully mastered the 2× table she was counting correctly in twenties, which had become very meaningful to her, having discovered she could collect 20-cent coins from supermarket trolleys which had been abandoned, especially during inclement weather.

There were two kinds of knowledge which were compartmentalized for Alice. There was maths which was an integral part of everyday life which she did not appear to know she knew, and maths divorced from real life which she found hard to comprehend. Whatever is done in school to make maths 'concrete' for primary school children, it must remain largely abstract simply because it does not relate to anything immediately real in the child's world. Problems are contrived – 'Imran sells his modem to Kylie for

. . .'. Or there are so-called 'concrete' activities which children have to undertake which rarely have practical relevance for them – measuring desks, counting cars, etc. Most concrete aids to teaching maths are themselves essentially abstract, number rods for example.

After laboriously extracting all the mathematical entries from the journal, the first thing I noticed was how chaotic it all was. Things are learned and forgotten. There are inexplicable advances and regressions. Progress is sometimes made without the apparent need for more basic prerequisite knowledge. Even though her mother assiduously notes down everything she can, Alice sometimes displays understanding of a concept without her mother having any idea how she acquired it. Perhaps some of Alice's learning was so apparently commonplace it even escaped her mother's close observation. For example, it is noted in the journal when she starts learning the time. Then, a year or so later she can tell the time accurately, even work out what the time will be one and three-quarters of an hour hence when something in the oven will be ready. But the journal contains very little in between which relates to learning to tell the time.

Alice's mother remarked that much learning appeared inconsequential and that it was only when she looked back that strands of learning appeared and patterns emerged. Alice seems, unconsciously, to extend what she knows by incorporating new ideas and concepts which dovetail into and extend her existing knowledge. She is the one who decides, subconsciously, when to concentrate, practise what she already knows, try something difficult, or repetitively go over something she has already learned in order to consolidate it. Little effort is wasted because what she is learning is embedded in her everyday activities. Sometimes she does play around with number patterns and relationships, demonstrating she is in fact beginning to get a grasp of the abstract properties of mathematics. But this is mostly at her own instigation.

It is worth stressing that being largely in control of her own learning does not mean that Alice is left to her own devices. Just as nearly all parents do with their children in the early years, her mother takes advantage of the many opportunities for extending her daughter's knowledge. If maths comes into it, it is included. It is guided participation, much of it through naturally occurring conversation related to everyday practical activities.

In a sentence, children in school learn maths by doing maths whereas Alice learns most of her maths when she is doing something else.

ALICE LEARNING MATHS [21]

Most people think of home educating parents as having all the time in the world to devote to their children but most have other children at home or in school, as well as housework. This particular mother had only one child, Alice, at home. In addition, however, throughout all but the final couple of months of the period of two-and-a-half years covered by the journal, she also looked after her granddaughter for five days a week from 7.30 a.m. to 5.30 p.m. The granddaughter was just three months old at the start of the journal.

The amount of material in the journal is daunting. It would require a book in itself to adequately describe and analyse Alice's progress in informal learning. The journal consists of closely written notes in exercise books with writing on both sides of the page.

The whole pile stands knee-high. And maths is just one small part of it. Days (and pages upon pages of the journal) go by without a mention of anything involving maths.

Alice's progress in understanding money will be illustrated in the following way. First, nearly all the entries which contain maths during the first two months will be described, except for those related to money. This will give some idea of the breadth of her learning experiences and also serve to establish a baseline. One of the reasons for the latter is to demonstrate just how little maths Alice knows at the start of the journal and that she therefore has very little general mathematical knowledge to transfer to learning about money. The second section will examine, step by step, Alice's progress in handling money, from August 1994 to December 1995, except for a break in the journal from October to December 1994. There is no protocol for recording informal learning at home. Alice's mother has to learn as she goes along.

ESTABLISHING A BASELINE: AUGUST TO OCTOBER 1994

Maths in context: cooking

Day One: 5 August 1994

Alice is a few days short of her seventh birthday. She and her mother are preparing five kilos of dried fruit for a wedding cake for Alice's aunt.

M: I'm going to weigh the cherries first. We need 500 grams.
A: (Looking at the scales) I can't see that. Where's that number?
M: Well, it doesn't have 375g written. We have to find it. 375g's just before 400g. It's a bit less than 400g.
A: (Pointing) Is this 400? This one with a 4 and two zeros?
M: (Pointing) Yes, and this is about 375g.
[talk moves on to tasting the fruit]
M: Will you cut the apricots up?
A: How small?
M: Oh, cut them into quarters first.
A: How? I can't make quarters.
M: Can you make halves?
A: (laughs) Of course I can. Just chop 'em in two (she demonstrates).
M: OK, well quarters are lots of four. How can we make apricots into four pieces?
A: (Looks intently at the apricot she cut in half) Oh, cut the halves in half! (begins happily chopping).
[later in the day]
M: We need 1½ kilograms of sultanas.
A: (Searching scales) This says 1 kilo. That's it isn't it? Kg is kilogram.
M: Yes, but we have one kilogram plus a half kilogram.
A: Well it doesn't say that. We can't do that one.
M: Yes we can. You find where it says 2 kilograms.
A: Yes, it's right round here. Here it is.
M: Well, that extra half a kilogram is half-way between one and two kilograms.
A: (Points to 400g past the 1kg mark) It's here. Is it just here?
M: Almost. Half a kilogram is 500 grams.
A: Four, five, six ... 400, 500, 600. It's the same! It's the same. It's 400, 500, 600, but they didn't put the number.
M: That's right. 500 grams is just between 400 and 600. That mark is for 500.

A: (Pouring sultanas on to the scale pan, sings) 200, 300, 400, 500, 600, 700, 800, that's how it goes.

[much later and a few pages on in the journal]

M: We've still got to do the prunes. 375 grams of pitted prunes. That means without the pips.

[talk moves on to a different topic]

A: (Changing the subject) Where do we have to go up to?

M: 375 grams. Where's that?

A: I don't know.

M: Just below the 400.

[later]

M: What have we been measuring the fruit in?

A: The scales.

M: Yes, and what are they marked out in?

A: Kilajoules or centres or something.

M: No, grams and kilograms.

A: Grams and kilograms.

M: Yes, they are for weight. The fruit is solid. Now, see the bottle over there? Can you read what's in that bottle?

A: (Sounding it out first) Tolley's brandy.

M: Right.

A: Sorry, I'm not drinking it!

M: It's to go in with the fruit. Can you find a number to tell us how much is in there?

A: Yes. Here it is. Here. Is it 375m one?

M: Yes, 375ml. That means mls. What sort of things are measured in mls?

A: I don't know.

M: Here's a clue. The baby's milk is measured in mls.

A: (Blank look)

M: Well, the brandy is measured in mls, so is the milk, and water can be too.

A: (Breaking in) Oh, I know. They're all drinks – um stuff, you know, liquid. They're all liquids.

M: What are you going to do with that plastic cup with the pips?

A: I'm going to weigh them. Can I weigh them on the scales?

M: OK, how much?

A: Nearly 200.

M: 200 what?

A: Um, kilometres or something.

M: Grams, 200 grams.

A: Grrrrrrrrrr!

After writing the notes taken during the course of the day she adds:

Note that the time period covered is just over 4 hours [from 11.45 a.m.]. Also, the time was broken up with the usual phone calls, caring for [the baby], a quick lunch, etc.

So, what can be said about this first day's recorded maths? First, it is almost certainly not the sum total of Alice's mathematical experiences for the day. Lots of other instances, sometimes very fleeting ones, might have gone unrecorded. Nor do we know what went on in her head – she may have given some thought to some of the above or to some other aspect of number. Second, what is recorded takes up very little time, no more than a few minutes in total. Third, all the maths was in the context of making a cake. If Alice had been asked what she had done during the day she would almost certainly have mentioned helping to make a wedding cake.

And what does the day tell us about Alice's mathematical knowledge? She has difficulty in reading whole hundreds but does start to grasp that whole hundreds increase as do single digits. She does not seem to understand the more complex 'a hundred and ... '. She does know about halves and seems to grasp quarters. She is not conversant with the terms grams and kilograms, but she does appreciate that liquids are measured in a different way.

Maths in context: on the road

The following excerpt concerns a car journey from Hobart to Launceston and back, from the south coast to the north coast of Tasmania. Note that in Tasmania there are distance markers which decrease in amounts of five kilometres, each preceded by the first letter of the main destination, in this case, L 120, L 115 ...

3 September 1994

M: See that number? How slow am I meant to go?
A: Eighty?
M: Yes.

M: See that sign? L 145. Launceston 145 kms. Those signs are every five kms. The numbers will get smaller and smaller as we get closer to Launceston.

(M: Whenever I was aware of one, I pointed it out and said the number. At last, when we got to the ones in the forties she began reading them for herself and could anticipate which one would come next)

M: What's that number ... one, one, zero?
A: One hundred and ten.
M: There are more coming up now we are getting close to Launceston.
A: Eighty, you have to do eighty. Now, sixty.
M: Yes I have to slow right down to sixty to go through the city.

Alice can recognize 80, 60 and 110. About two weeks before this Alice asked her mother, in the supermarket, if 2 with 5 made 25. Now somehow or other she can recognize numbers descending in fives from 45. She has also gained a first understanding of compound numbers over a hundred, being able to recognize 110.

Two days later, on the return journey, Alice continued to grapple with and extend her knowledge of compound numbers, mainly related to road distances. Here is just one short excerpt from the journal covering the journey home. It shows, too, how one topic can lead to another.

5 September 1994

M: Overtaking lane 300 metres.
A: What's 300?
M: Three and two zeros.
A: Three hundred and twenty?
M: No, three, double zero.
A: What does double mean?
M: It means two of anything. If you went to Sizzlers and had two of a pudding, you'd be having a double pudding.

A: And if you had double double you'd have four puddings. And if you had double double double, you'd have six puddings.

M: Yes, I suppose you would.

Incidental learning

There were many opportunities for incidental learning. During the journey just described, Alice's mother drew her attention to the cardinal compass points, in reference to the sun in their eyes and the rising and setting sun. Alice did not seem to take it in, though she did understand that North-East would be between North and East. They also stopped at a bridge built by convicts in 1836. Alice's attention was drawn to the date of the bridge written in Roman numerals. There was a milestone with distances to Hobart and Launceston also in Roman numerals.

The next excerpt illustrates an essential aspect of incidental learning, having an adult on hand to point out things of interest and suggest activities which might catch the child's attention. They are visiting a nearby bird hide.

1 September 1994

[On the way to the bird hide]

A: What's that 'V' for?

M: It's an indicator for some sort of cable. It shows how far down it is. Six feet. That's an old measurement. One foot is as long as a school ruler. The idea for a foot was that it was as long as a man's foot. Why wasn't it very useful to use a man's foot for a measure?

A: One man's foot might be this long and another man's foot would be this long (indicating with her hands). And the man who decided it, only his foot would be the right size.

M: Yes, so they made a standard measurement which was named one foot.

A: There's another dead rabbit ...

[On the way back]

M: What do you think that sign says?

A: F.P. Fire pump.

M: Yes, fire pump. Where they can plug in the fire hoses.

A: I already know that.

M: But thank you for telling me! How far does it say? How many metres?

A: Eighty, no, 18 metres.

M: 1.8 metres.

A: Oh, the dot in the middle means point then.

Alice has certainly learned some maths, without any lessons, certainly not from her point of view. The following examples, all occurring during the course of a single day, show again how important it is to have an adult on hand to respond and to encourage further learning. She is also doing her own maths course, in her head.

7 September 1994

[In the car]

A: Those numbers on that bus add up to 10.

M: Yes, that's right. And what is the number they make standing side by side?

A: One hundred and forty-five.

M: Yes, well done. That's the number of the bus. Bus number one hundred and forty-five.

[Walking past a shop]

A: What's one point zero zero?

M: It's one dollar.

A: Are you buying that ruler for me?

M: Yes. I know you already have a ruler, but this one has the cms marked out very clearly. It'll help you learn the cms.

(M: Alice comes over to have a closer look. She counts the cms from 0 to 30)

[On the way home in the car]

A: It's six years until I'm 13.

M: Well done, to work that out.

A: I did it with add ups in my head. I like to do lots of add ups and take aways in my head.

The following are further recorded fragments of maths, mostly embedded in other activities, which may have contributed to learning during this two-month period. The mention of tessellations follows on from a visit to a tessellated pavement on the coast.

- at breakfast she worked out that $1\frac{1}{2}$ cups for porridge was the same as three half cups.
- while making bread she adjusted the oven temperature and timer.
- there was talk of tessellations leading to six triangles making up a hexagon. Later she sang:

    Hex-ex-ex-agon
    It's got six-six-six
    It's got six triangles in it
    It's a hex, hex, hexagon.
    Oh! The timer. My bread's cooked.

- she counted pairs of knobs on chairs up to 12.
- she struggled with working out how old she'll be when the baby is 6.
- she measured in cms, half cms and quarter cms.

LEARNING ABOUT MONEY: AUGUST 1994 TO DECEMBER 1995

Although Alice's mathematical knowledge has progressed, it is clear from the above that she does not know much maths which could be applied to dealing with money. We now go back to the beginning of the journal and trace Alice's learning about money during the course of 17 months.

Alice does not seem particularly interested in maths for its own sake, though she does make more or less normal progress according to checklists her mother uses to gauge what she has learned each year. With regard to money, however, she makes rapid progress. The reason may be that she has come to appreciate the critical link between money and possessions. As a consequence she realizes that her pocket money and savings have real, practical value. This leads her to extend her learning by totting up money she comes across in jars and her mother's purse. At first her mother does most of the counting, but Alice slowly takes over, with her mother gradually withdrawing as she moves towards mastery.

18 August 1994

[They are in the supermarket. Having failed to persuade her mother to allow her to spend her money on a lolly she compromises with buying fruit]

A: (Points to grapes) How much are these? It says it here. How much?

M: They're $5 a kilo, but that's a big bag full. You'd only want a little bunch like this. (I pick up a small bunch to show her)

A: How much would they cost?

M: Well, I can't say exactly because it's only a little part of a kilogram, but it wouldn't be more than a dollar.

A: (Turning from the grapes) Nup. (Picks up a mandarin) How much is one of these?

M: They're four for a dollar. That means one costs a quarter of a dollar, 25¢.

A: Mmmm. How much for two? Is two more than a dollar?

M: No, two cost half a dollar. That's 50¢.

A: (Opening her purse) Fifty cents. Is that one of these with the funny sides?

M: (I point to one in her purse) Yes, one of those. It's 50¢. It's half a dollar. It will buy two mandarins.

A: Nup. (Points to a kiwi fruit) That's a 2 and a 5. Is that 25? Is it? Is it 25 dollars?

M: Not dollars. You're right that it's 25, 25 cents.

A: Nope, I don't want one of those.

M: Alice, my arms are aching. You'll have to choose soon. The baby's getting heavy.

A: (Picks up an enormous Golden Delicious apple) How much is this? This is good. I'll have this.

M: They're 15¢ each. (Alice buys the apple. She takes a 20 cent coin confidently from her purse. She seems to know she doesn't need more than 20 cents)

If Alice had been asked what she did at the supermarket she might say her mother would not let her buy a lolly but that she bought a big apple instead. She would not say that she had learnt any maths.

It is obvious she knows very little about money. Whether she really does know that 20¢ is the coin to proffer for a 15¢ apple, as her mother thinks she might, is questionable. But the possibility she does understand should not be discounted – throughout the journal there are inexplicable advances in understanding and equally inexplicable regressions. As we see from this next entry she cannot yet 'read' money.

7 September 1994

[In the supermarket Alice wanted to buy some sweets with her pocket money]

A: How much is that one?

(M: I've always told her prices, but I realized that she could probably manage them herself now)

M: The one this side tells you the dollars. The ones this side are the cents. So, this is two dollars and how many cents?

A: Two dollars and 85 cents.

M: Yes, and they're really hot mints. I think they'd burn your mouth.

A: Can I have these?

M: No, those big packets are for birthday parties and things like that. I don't want you to buy a big one like that. Look over there. You'll find something suitable there.

A: How much is this one?

M: Well ... I think you can read them. Remember? The ones that side of the point are the cents.

A: 85 cents?

(She points to others)

A: One dollar and 75 cents.
M: M-hmm.
A: One dollar and 65 cents.

[Later]

Alice wants to count her pocket money. As might be expected from the above her mother has to do nearly all of it for her, though she is able to count single dollars.

(Alice has her pocket money all tipped out on the floor)
A: Will you count this for me?
M: OK.
(I pick up two 50¢ pieces. She still calls these the funny-sided ones)
Two of these make one dollar.
(I put them together and place them on the floor)
You get those other two 50¢ to make another dollar.
(She places the second dollar beside the first)
Now there are two dollars.
A: These three are single dollars aren't they.
M: Yes, put them in a row. That's 1, 2, 3, 4, 5 dollars. Now we can make a dollar with five of these twenties. So you've got three more dollars. How many dollars now?
A: Five and three more. It's eight.
M: You've got eight dollars. Now, what's left?
A: All these. Can we make more dollars with these?
M: Let's see. Three twenties – that's 60¢. Add 10 makes 70, add 10 makes 80. Two of these [5¢ coins] make 10 cents. That's 80 plus 10 is 90. Then five left over makes 95¢. So altogether you have 8 dollars and 95 cents.
A: That's a lot isn't it? Is that a lot?
M: Whether it's a lot or not depends on what you want to buy with it. If you want to buy a car it isn't enough to pay for the key. It would buy 17 × 50¢ bags of lollies and you'd have 45¢ change. It would buy a paperback book. And I know it was hard work saving that much.
A: It's quite a lot then.

In the above excerpt Alice's mother introduced her to 2 × 50¢ = $1. Now she seems to have grasped it for herself.

11 September 1994

M: (In the afternoon – I am trying to have a rest because we pick up someone from the airport at 10 p.m. tonight. Alice hops up onto the bed and empties the contents of her purse on the bed to count. She has hit it hard over the weekend)
A: Will you help me count this please?
M: All right, spread it all out.
A: Wait. There's two of these with the funny sides [50¢]. They make a dollar together. Then this is a dollar. That's two dollars.
(She picks up a $2 coin and thinks for a while)
A: This one has two dollars hasn't it? That's 1, 2, 3 … four dollars. Now there are a few of these (hesitates).
M: Put that there. That's 20¢ plus 10 is 30, plus 10 is …
A: Forty cents.
M: Plus ten.
A: Fifty cents.
(This is the best effort she's made in counting money)

She is beginning to make discernible progress in understanding how to count and handle money. She can count half dollars, recognize $2 coins and seemingly counts in tens.

[Gap in journal from October to December, 1994]

Two to three months later Alice is seriously in the business of getting to know about money. It is assuming greater importance in her life . . .

18 December 1994

> [Mother writes] Xmas presents. She has $2 for each present. Wants to buy one for 50¢ – realizes she could get two for $1. Then 'There's $2. That's got four 50¢. I could get four of them.'

1995

. . . but she has not made progress on all fronts. Her advance is untidy to say the least. In this next excerpt she does not know immediately what 50 + 10 make – even suggesting they make 100. She can count up in tens if prompted but cannot calculate 50 plus 10 without counting up in tens from zero. She also thinks that 70 and 5 make 80! She is either struggling or just not concentrating . . .

9 January 1995

> A: How much have I got?
> M: How many whole dollars?
> A: 2.
> M: Now, what's this one?
> A: 50¢ (no longer funny-sided ones).
> M: What's this?
> A: 10¢.
> M: So . . . 50 and 10.
> A: I don't know. 100?
> M: Count in tens and find out what's 10 more than 50.
> A: 10, 20 . . . 100.
> M: You've got 50. See? This is 10. So you have to add 10 to 50. You have to find out what is 10 more than 50. So count again in tens and stop when you get to 10 after 50.
> A: 10, 20 . . . 60, that's it.
> M: Now what are these?
> A: They're 5s.
> M: Two of them make another ten. So what's ten more than 60?
> A: 10, 20 . . . 70, 70 cents.
> M: Right, now just add another 5.
> A: 80?
> M: It's only one five. It takes two fives to make 10.
> A: It's 70 and 5 more.
> M: Yes.
> A: 75. So I've got $2 and 75 cents.

. . . and things do not get better when she is tired though she does now know that two 5¢ coins make 10¢ . . .

3 February 1995

A: Help me count my money please Mum.
M: OK. Which pieces of money are worth the most?
A: (Points to $5 notes)
M: What are they?
A: $5.
M: How many have you got?
A: Two. That's $10 ... $11 ... $12. But now I can't add up the rest.
M: OK. Put $12 together. Now, what's worth most out of the rest?
A: This.
M: What's it called?
A: 50¢ (sings a song about 50¢).
M: Aren't we counting your money?
A: Oh yes. I was just singing.
M: How many lots of 10 have you got?
A: I don't know.
M: Well, look.
A: (sings)
M: ... I can only give you a few more minutes.
A: Three 10s because the two fives make a 10.
M: OK. What's 50 add on three 10s?
A: (counting on fingers) 39.
M: How could it be 39?
A: 50. I was adding on three 10s.
M: Look, Alice. 50, 60, 70, 80. Then you've got five more to add on. $12.85.
A: (crying) You're just tricking me.
M: No, it is $12.85, but we are both too tired to do this tonight.

... but suddenly, over the next ten days, it all comes together without anything obvious happening in between. Something has been going on in Alice's head without her being deliberately or even informally taught, at least as far as being recorded in the journal is concerned ...

13 February 1995

A: I've got $2 and some of the shiny ones. Have I got as much as another dollar here?
M: Maybe, count it up.
(A spreads coins out on floor. She uses 5s, 10, and 20s to build up two lots of 50)
A: 50 and 50 make a dollar. So I have got another dollar. I've got 3 dollars. And there's a 20 and a 5 left over – 25. $3 and 25 cents.

It would be so easy to assume on the basis of this that if Alice knows that a mixture of 5¢ and 10¢ coins make 50¢ and that two 50¢ coins make a dollar that she will know that 100¢ also does. But she has not fully grasped this until her mother brings her attention to it ...

14 February 1995

A: I can count this up to a dollar. Look. Two 20s add on 10. That's a funny-sided one [50¢].
Put it with this 50¢ and it's a dollar. Two 50s make 100 cents.
M: And what do you have if you have a 100 cents?

A: I don't know. Oh, a dollar.

Although Alice still knows relatively little about money she is not lacking in confidence when it comes to dealing with a shop assistant. Moreover, she accepts without loss of face when the assistant points out she has made a mistake. There is no feeling of being 'wrong'. There is very little sense of failure throughout the journal when she makes a mistake. Perhaps it is because it is not dealt with in the same way that failing to solve a problem in school is. The shop assistant does not even mention she has miscalculated, only that she has not got enough money for two chocolates at 35¢ each. It is just part of the process of learning to buy things in a shop . . .

7 March 1995

(Looking at chocolate frogs in a chemist's shop)
A: How much are all these please?
Asst.: Those plain ones are 25¢ each and all the ones with cream centres are 35¢ each.
A: I've got 50¢ so I can buy one of these (plain) and one of these (cream centre).
Asst.: No, you haven't got enough. You could buy two of these though.
M: The plain ones are 25¢ each. Two lots of 25 add up to 50¢. You could get one cream one and have some change, or you could get two plain ones for exactly 50¢.
(She chooses two plain ones)

Again, Alice's knowledge of handling money is extended in a situation which has practical relevance for her.

17 March 1995

(M writes: She compares prices in 'Chicken Feed' [shop] to see what she can buy without breaking into her $5 note)

Alice is now competent at adding silver to make a dollar, even to the extent of recognizing that five 20¢ coins make $1 . . .

19 March 1995

(Puts a 10¢ beside two 5¢, then lines up four 20¢)
A: I've got a dollar of change! See! One, two, three, four, five. These make a twenty and there's four other twenties. See? Five 20s make up to $1.

[later]
(M writes: Relative left behind some change. Alice came across it – 6 × 10, 4 × 5 and 1 × 20 and added it up correctly declaring it was exactly a dollar)

Now to an inexplicable regression. Suddenly, Alice does not seem to know that 50¢ must be more than 35¢. From what we have seen so far she appears to have grasped it at a conceptual level. But there may a condition, for all Alice knows, perhaps related to prices, under which this does not apply. Perhaps the logical necessity of 50¢ being more than 35¢ is not fully incorporated into Alice's understanding of 'more than'. Whatever the explanation, it does serve to demonstrate how difficult it is to know exactly how a child's cognitive understanding progresses ...

4 April 1995

(In supermarket, Alice shows me a 50¢ piece)
A: Is 35¢ less or more than this?
M: Is 35 more than 50 or less than 50? Which is the biggest?
A: 50¢.
M: Yes, that's right.
A: Can I get two 35¢ lollies with this?
M: No, only one and you'll get some change.

She demonstrates that now she really does grasp that 100¢ = $1 ...

10 April 1995

A: Five dollars plus 100¢ makes six dollars doesn't it?

And she is not lacking in confidence ...

3 May 1995

A: 200¢. That's $2. Did you know that?
M: Yes, you're right.

In a visit to the supermarket they compare brands of washing powders and honey in which the only apparent difference is in the price. Alice's mother points out that honey is just honey. Alice is astonished at the price difference. This may not advance Alice's cognitive understanding but it does reinforce the importance of money in real everyday life and therefore helps to further Alice's motivation to understand how to use it. Alice is learning an essential life skill, how to shop in the real world, and shopping involves using and understanding money.

Alice is now able to count relatively large amounts of money, and can add dollars and cents, but she has a problem with the apparently easy step of adding on remaining cents to whole dollars when the amount is large.

26 June 1995

[Alice counts a heap of change in her mother's purse. She stacked 5¢ correctly but came unstuck when she got to 20¢ coins which she treated as 10¢, until the error was pointed out. She worked correctly up to $21 but was unsure what to do with the rest. She needed help to count the remainder yielding a total of $21.45]

Repetition and drill may be important for learning maths in school, and this may be the case for informal learning too, only in the latter case it is the child who decides when and what needs rehearsing. Because Alice takes the decision she is cognitively much more engaged in the occupation. Here she rehearses, more confidently, and in a new way, her understanding that 100¢ = $1.

29 June 1995

> (M writes: [Alice] spontaneously writes 10¢, 20¢ ... $1)
> A: See. Not 100. It's cents, so it's a dollar. That's 100 cents.

Back to whole dollars and remaining cents. Her mother is perplexed by Alice's inability to add on left-over cents. It highlights the findings with regard to learning maths described in Chapter 2, that blocks to learning can be extremely idiosyncratic and difficult for an adult (whether parent or teacher) to comprehend. But again, she does not get anything 'wrong'. It is more a question of going on till you get it right. Her mother helps her to do so, making for increased confidence rather than denting it.

9 July 1995

> (M writes) Alice counts all the change in the housekeeping money: $14.40. Her only problem was with the left-over 40¢. Goodness knows why.

31 July 1995

> A counts all the money in the home ed. jar up to $50 with no problem.

During the next two months there is not a single mention of money. Yet there is progress. Alice's troublesome difficulty with adding remaining cents to whole dollars disappears. These next two excerpts also serve to highlight, yet again, the difference between knowledge related to the real world of savings which can be used to make actual purchases and that which is out of context, lotto 'add ups'. It is experience of maths in the real world which contributed to Alice's understanding.

29 September 1995

> (M writes) She added up her savings correctly: $31.60 ... She did this remarkably quickly compared with simple lotto add ups which she often got wrong.

Alice is not at all bothered by her mistakes. She simply enlists the help of her mother to rectify them. There is no sense of being 'wrong'.

4 October 1995

> (A has $2 pay to add to her savings)
> A: Mum, come and count. I keep making mistakes.
> M: $33.60.

A: That's what I got. But it must be wrong. Last time it was $21.60.
M: $10 from [a friend].
A: Oh yes ... 21, 31, then my $2 pay. I'm going to spend the 60¢. Then I'll still have $33.

12 December 1995 [end of year assessment]

(M writes) End of year – Rigby maths Grade 2 checklist [Alice's age level]. Only two things can't do, months of year in sequence and time in $\frac{1}{4}$ and $\frac{1}{2}$s ... Her competence [with money] just through shopping, comparing prices, etc., goes way beyond what is required in this list. The assessment requires giving change for any amount up to 20¢. I'm not sure she could do this. But there is nothing you can buy up to 20¢. The cheapest item she's bought is 35¢.

Again, this highlights the difference between real and abstract, out of context, learning in school. It is assumed that because children have difficulty in subtracting from amounts greater than 20 they will therefore find calculating change from more than 20¢ equally difficult. But as we see with Alice, the two skills are compartmentalized. It must eventually be easier to move from knowledge of maths gained through real and meaningful experience with money to more abstract maths rather than the other way round, as is inevitably the case with most maths in school. Having said this, it has to be acknowledged that Alice does not yet find it easy to transfer her knowledge of maths, gained from handling money, to more abstract maths as in maths lotto.

POSTSCRIPT: A YEAR LATER

Now that Alice can deal with money competently, at least as far as shopping and her savings are concerned, there is little mention of money calculations during 1996 though during this year she has continued to make progress. She is now approaching $9\frac{1}{2}$ years of age. Here are just a few examples.

2 January 1997

(M: Alice and Dad were looking in a K-Mart catalogue. There were lamps priced at $39.95 each and marked as a saving of $10.00 on the usual price)
A: Oh, then their usual price must be $49.95.

In the meantime, too, she has learned and forgotten 'carrying'.

17 January 1997

(M: Alice counts her liquid assets once again: $57.45)
M: Let's see how much you'll have in your bank once it's put in.
(I write it out)
  270.29 (in bank)
+ 57.45

(She begins adding on the left-hand side)
M: Start right over here Alice.
(She's forgotten what to do with the carried ones, but soon catches on again)
A: $327.74. That's a heap!

Although she gets the next calculation wrong, her growing mental agility in arithmetic is obvious, as her mother notes.

21 January 1997

A: If we bought each of [my friends] a book and recorder like mine, it would cost her $43
   and 85¢ because they're $14.95 each.
M: Umm. I'd do the 10s first.
A: (Cutting in) That's what I did.
M: Three 10s are 30. Three 4s are 12. That's $42. Each lot of 95¢ is just 5¢ less than a dollar,
   so I'll take three lots of 5¢ off $3.
A: That's 85¢.
M: Almost. Two dollars and 85 cents. So that's 44 dollars and 85 cents altogether. You
   were only out by one dollar and that was a hard one to do in your head.
(M writes: . . . I'm pleased with all this. This is shaping up to be far better than the last diary
already)

But her knowledge can still desert her in a new situation . . .

22 January 1997

(A has found a jar of [obsolete] 1 and 2 cent coins)
A: How many of these make a dollar.
M: Think of what cent means. Cents.
(Blank look from A)
One hundred.
A: Oh yes, 100¢ to make up a $1. Do you think there's 100 here?
M: I've no idea.
(She begins piling them in 10 cent piles)
M: How many piles of 10 cents do you need to make a dollar?
A: A hundred. Oh no, it's 10. Ten lots of ten cents.
M: That's right.

12 February 1997

[The family is about to sell some articles through a shop which charges 20 per cent
commission for selling them. They expect the sale to realize about $700. Alice can now
estimate what this means in general terms of a fraction and exactly in terms of a
percentage]
A: Won't they get most of the money?
Father: 20 per cent.
M: Do you know what 20 per cent means Alice?
A: Ummm.
M: How much is 20 per cent of a dollar?
A: Gee. About a quarter. Twenty cents out of every dollar.

And here is more concrete evidence of this kind of understanding . . .

26 February 1997

(A third of a dollar came up. Alice said straight away it was about 30¢. So I said that was only a third of 90¢. Alice said 'Oh 33¢, not quite')
M: And divide the last cent in 3.
A: $33\frac{1}{3}$.
M: Yes, and what's a third of a 100?
A: $33\frac{1}{3}$ because there are 100 cents in a dollar.

What does Alice's experience of learning about money teach us about informal learning? First and foremost there is no doubt that it works. Alice kept up with her school peers in general and progressed way past them with regard to handling money, with a great deal less time and effort than would have been required in school. The increments in her learning are plainly visible. Second, it teaches us that not even maths learning need proceed in a logical sequence. Even with the detailed descriptions provided it is difficult to 'see' the process of informal learning as it happens, with its inexplicable headways and backslidings. It may be possible to break down mathematical knowledge logically in planning the curriculum, but children do not have to follow the logic in order to progress. Third, Alice's experiences highlight the idiosyncratic nature of learning. She needs to put her own construction on the new knowledge which confronts her, as if she is putting into practice her own theory of learning. This idea is developed further in Chapter 11.

Although informal learning is nothing like learning in school, it does meet most of the requirements for teaching excellence. The situations in which learning takes place have real meaning for Alice so that her interest and motivation to learn are aroused. Mistakes have no negative overtones. They simply serve as signposts in the direction of the next step in learning. She is able to regress, as she often does, without concern or loss of face. Most important of all, she has a mentor who is always on hand to guide her, to draw her attention to mathematical aspects of situations, to get her over difficult steps, taking over when necessary and leaving alone when appropriate.

At the beginning of this chapter I drew attention to Alice's mother's lack of ideological commitment to, and her occasional misgivings about, informal education. Towards the end of the journal she had become much more optimistic.

18 December 1996

I looked through a [borrowed] maths Grade 3 Teachers' Manual ... Most of it was stuff contrived to teach in a classroom, concepts Alice has picked up in her day-to-day life ...

Chapter 9

Literacy

The main focus of the book is on learning in general. However, two additional themes also emerged: the acquisition of literacy and social development (dealt with in Chapter 10).

It is generally assumed that the advent of universal schooling led to a marked increase in literacy during the second half of the nineteenth century. Yet, even at the beginning of the nineteenth century it has been estimated that at least a half of males and a third of females were literate. The rapid growth in popular literature during the latter part of the eighteenth and early nineteenth centuries could not have taken place without a substantially literate populace. Some learned in Sunday or village schools but many children ...

> ... learned to read and sometimes to write, from their parents, relatives, friends or neighbours, in various informal settings and at times convenient to other tasks. (Harrison, 1988, p. 228)

Although the teaching of reading has since become a highly professionalized activity, there is no reason whatsoever why home educating parents should not be able to do it. After all, many parents teach their children to read at home before they go to school. Still, it is a crucial accomplishment for every child and it is natural that home educating parents should experience some misgivings about undertaking the task. As it turned out, few reported any serious problems except those who took their children out of school because they were failing to learn to read. So it is not so much a question of whether they can. Of far greater interest is the way parents go about the task. As we shall see, few rely on a single reading scheme or a specific approach. They find that responding to children as individual learners is far more important.

In school, children who have not learned to read by the age of 7 are generally classified as having special needs. Although few parents came across any serious problems, it was quite startling to encounter a significant number of children who had not learned to read by the age of 7 or even much later. Their parents were naturally worried at the time, though as it turned out they need not have been. Surprisingly, there was no adverse effect on subsequent literacy because, in general, these 'late' reading children quickly caught up with and passed the level of reading commensurate with their age and went on to thoroughly enjoy reading. This is in marked contrast with late reading children in school, who typically fall further behind their chronological reading age as they progress through the primary school.

Finally, children who are educated at home have much more time to read for pleasure, which most do enthusiastically. Parents' descriptions of their children's reading for enjoyment read like a celebration of literacy.

LEARNING TO READ

Learning to read is as important a milestone in a child's life as learning to walk or talk. To be unable to read is to be socially and intellectually maimed for life. Learning to read is rightly at the top of the educational agenda for parents and teachers alike.

The concern with literacy has spawned an enormous research and professional literature, a plethora of methods of teaching reading and bitter controversies about the merits of different approaches. In school, infant teachers have the main responsibility for the task and are generally expected to have completed it by the time the children are 7. This age is generally regarded as critical and reading specialists are usually available to give extra help to those children still experiencing difficulty.

When a child in school fails to learn to read, the problem is located in the child or the child's background. For home educated children, by contrast, it is the parents who will almost certainly bear the burden of responsibility for failure. Their concern with literacy is probably the greater because of this and is further heightened by their lack of professional training.

> He's beginning ... to read. But some children are much more fluent than him. I tried some reading but it was always a battle. I'd end up shouting. The underlying fear is that you are jeopardizing their future. [87]

Nevertheless, the children in the study generally learned to read without serious difficulty. Interest therefore shifts from whether home educating parents are able to teach their children to read to the light which their experiences throw on the process of learning to read and on the development of literacy in general.

It might be expected that the parents would make up for their lack of professional knowledge with the individual attention they can offer their children and this turned out to be the case. Although they made use of schemes and methods commonly used in school, how they used them was determined by what worked with the individual child. There were often marked differences between children in the same family. What worked with one child did not with a sibling. The process for each child could also be dynamic and change over time. Such an individualized approach would simply be impractical in the classroom, but not at home.

Heated debates among reading researchers and teachers about the teaching of reading are not mirrored among home educators, whose approach is much more pragmatic. Although preferences were stated these were very much tempered by feedback from children's progress. Overall it is the sheer variety of approaches, including some rather unusual ones, which is striking. Another interesting feature is that it is the children, rather than the parents, who often dictate the propitious moment to advance reading, in the context of something that has attracted their interest.

The following attempt to classify is therefore somewhat arbitrary. Parents might be better described as finding out how best to teach their children to read rather than simply implementing a given scheme or method, in other words, a problem-solving approach.

First are some examples of using and adapting a mainly phonic approach.

Reading is so important, the earlier the better. I like the phonic approach – we kept it up for some time with her. She now attempts every word because of her training with phonics. [80]

I used phonics ... I don't want to start early, before they're interested. It's more difficult then. Learning will happen quicker when they're interested ... We got hold of old-fashioned readers. She could read long words just because she could sound out the letters. It made me realize phonics are so important, flowing well from simple to complex. [44]

I didn't sit down to teach her to read ... but I knew to concentrate on phonics, sounds, at 4 to 5. [52]

Basically, it's phonics, but they grow out of them, i.e. after the 'beginning stages' other methods seem to be incorporated, e.g. sight recognition, formation of words, syllables, etc. [28]

We ... started with the phonic approach: pig, fig, etc. He got sick of this and now we are learning to read with a simple book on Australian animals. He thinks this is great. He thinks that a lot of the modern readers are silly. These books on Australian animals give him information. [2]

He's not reading properly yet, but he's just clicked on to the sound of letters, all phonetically. It's a useful way of teaching preliminaries. And I use flash cards with pictures. He's getting much better at letter recognition. Using the computer has helped to trigger him off with letter sounds. [57]

Here are some who preferred a mainly visual approach.

With [him] I started getting and using books, flash cards, letters, and a reading scheme. [45]

I didn't do phonics etc. – but whole word – she learned that way. Six months ago she started looking at comic books, started looking at them and reading bits of them. Now she sometimes reads aloud, leaving out words she doesn't know. She's done the last bit of learning to read herself. It suddenly just happened that she'd got it! I was a bit scared of being too 'teachery', but she just read ... You can read! She realized what she could do and was quite pleased. [66]

At eight months she wanted to make sense out of books. I used flash cards. As she got older I started with phonics, then Look and Say. It worked so quickly I used it with all the others. They could read cat before they could do 'Kuh-ah-tuh'. [91]

I had lots of books, Ladybird books thrown out of school for burning. He just wasn't interested in reading at first, but I could tell he was ready, e.g. he knew all the magnetic letters he played with. One day he just went through the whole thing. He knew words in the Ladybird books but the content was not inspiring. He loved playing shops. I wrote the words on cards, all the vegetables. He must have learnt fifty words in a week, of foodstuffs. Again, it was a game. When he was younger he read the tins in the shops. Then I made cards with words like 'is' and 'and' and 'Daddy is happy'. Then I jumped into beginner books. He's always loved to be read to. There was no scheme – just one of those things that happened, just through feeling and intuition. He likes comics, but prefers to be read to. If we get a book out of the Library which I read – if he wants it a second time, e.g. 'Secret Seven', he has to read it himself, and he does. He loves the sports section in the paper, mostly for the scores. He was an excellent reader by 4. [99]

The first thing is they learn the alphabet from *Sesame Street*. They learn that a book tells a story. They learn the first letter of their names and then of other names. Then they write the alphabet. Then very simple words. Then they learn to spell out two- and three-letter words. They get interested from the start, just telling them stories. Also, before they could read or write we made a book with drawings. I wrote down what they'd said. They felt like they'd written a book then. [33]

So far, we have seen parents using and adapting methods as their children learned to read. Another approach was to allow for individual variation from the start by acquiring a range of materials and deliberately using mixed approaches.

I bought a whole mixture of things, using different methods, different approaches. [25]

I used all kinds of methods, books with photos with captions underneath. I labelled things, used phonics, look and say. It was spasmodic – not every day. The simpler stuff is condescending. It's well set out but she found it not intellectually stimulating enough. I tried a series but it was deadly dull and boring ... [24]

The following parents found that each child in the family needed a different approach.

The approach for every child for reading and writing is completely different. This contradicts school. The differences are dramatic. [One of them] could read when she was 3, as a result of my teaching, mainly using flash cards and playing flash card games. But I wouldn't do that again and I haven't with the others. [Another] learned entirely by herself. When I was a teacher I found this unbelievable. I honestly don't know how she learned. It still mystifies me. She never had any formal teaching in reading. She still picks up words way beyond her. [The other two] both learned the alphabet and used phonics, putting words together. I'm a great believer in phonics, but it's not the only programme. I believe in all sorts of things – strike while the iron's hot, that they should experience as few failures as possible ... [3]

It fascinates me how different they all are from each other. One will learn with a graded system, another with a different one and some will refuse the whole lot. They are as individual as children learning to walk and talk ... [One] was a spontaneous reader, at 4, without being taught. I bought her books to help her learn to read. She didn't need them. She read them straight off ... [She] learned by osmosis ... With [another] my approach has been to use standard methods. [One] had difficulty. We couldn't teach him. But he loved being read to. When he was 9 he realized what he'd learned by heart correlated with the page and he took off in one go. [With one daughter] we battled with little light at the end of the tunnel. She could not read till 11. It was difficult for her. After her eleventh birthday she took off. Over the next two years she read everything she could lay her hands on. We did our best not to let it bother her. It only did so momentarily. She's still not a natural speller. It was simple dyslexia. [31]

All the children in school are individuals. My two children learned to read very differently. In school they use a method. At home you can teach children as they need. [My daughter] taught herself to read, always asking me to write and draw – by $1\frac{1}{2}$ she knew dozens of words, always asking for me to read letters, e.g. on the fridge. By 18 months she knew the whole alphabet phonetically. [My son] was different and more demanding. I taught him phonetically. He got the alphabet by 3, then [I used] Ladybird at 4 when I noticed that he was not progressing by himself. [69]

These insights into learning to read raise the question of to what extent some children in school may fall behind simply because they are not given individual attention. Inevitably, some children will not be suited to blanket methods which are teacher-directed. A single method shown to result in better outcomes than another, when large numbers of children are compared, conceals the fact that certain children will be casualties of any given scheme or approach which does not suit their individual learning styles.

Further evidence of the complexity of the acquisition of basic literacy is that some children learn to read without their parents being able to explain how. One example was given above. Here are some more.

> When she learned to read, it just came. We'd read books together and I'd help her with difficult words. [61]

> [The older two boys] learned in school. The other children just picked it up. We read a lot. [18]

> [One of them] is making up stories. This is the precursor of reading. It's part of taking control of the situation. Then it just happens. [64]

> She learned to read by listening to [her older sister]. I never taught her to read. She just did. [73]

> I started with phonics; he was not interested. People asked if he could read. I got worried. Then in September he just read, including long words. Since then he reads really well. [43]

Of course a few children did experience difficulty.

> [My younger son] found reading daunting. He had moderate dyslexia; a great deal of difficulty. I thought he'd grow out of it ... If things got difficult he'd just give up. I never worried about it. He would do marvellous invented spelling. [54]

> [My younger son, aged 8] can read but not that well. We've always felt we are pushing up hill. He gets confused with saw/was and back/black and finds 'blue' difficult. Perhaps he needs a different scheme. We'd pushed with him. Then we didn't bother till he acted. One day he wanted to read and he went through three books in half an hour, the ones he'd been struggling with before. He gets upset if he feels he's failing. We are now on a plateau with reading again. He likes looking at picture-based library books. [98]

There were two children with severe learning difficulties associated with neurological disabilities. Apart from these, as far as could be ascertained, just one child had serious problems which had not been overcome by 11 years of age. Who knows if she would have learned more easily in school? Her parents had already withdrawn her elder sister from school, partly because she, too, had experienced difficulties in reading.

> [One daughter, aged 11] was slow. She's still a very poor reader. She guesses – it doesn't have to make sense for her. [45]

There were occasions when children were withdrawn from school partly because of reading difficulties. A rather startling example is of a girl taken out of school because at nearly 8 she could not read and was failing badly in other areas. The school recommended placement in a special school. Her mother, after taking her out of school, went 'back to basics' as she put it. Within 18 months at home her daughter could read 'any book off the shelf' and was also reading for pleasure.

> [My daughter, now aged 11] reads adult things. We are reading *Wind in the Willows* together.
> [Daughter] I like the Nancy Drew mysteries. I spend hours reading. I can get through a book in a day. I take a lot out of the library at a time. [98]

Parents can obviously teach their children to read without professional training. This is not to question the professionalism in the teaching of reading in school where the teacher has to draw on a range of strategies to maximize progress for 30 or so children who are all at different stages. But it underlines, in keeping with learning in general, that individual attention more than compensates for professional expertise.

'LATE' READERS

Webb (1990) cites an adult who was home educated and who remembers not having started learning to read until he was 8.

> I recall my mother trying to teach me to read when I was about five. It was hopeless – I just was not interested. I could have been bored with it to the point when it would have made it harder to learn later. Fortunately, she did not persist; she dropped it completely. Then when I was about eight years old I suddenly wanted to know how to read – I was fascinated by the printed word. At this point I would probably have been considered backward, even retarded in a regular school. But then I started learning to read. On my own. No formal 'lessons', no wishing I didn't have to do it ... by the time I was twelve I had reached a level of reading that even the education authorities agreed was that of an adult. (p. 90)

I assumed that this was one individual's particular experience. I was wrong.

Teachers acknowledge that children learn to read at different ages but there is great concern if the task of attaining basic literacy has not been accomplished by the age of 7 at the latest. They are right to be concerned. Children who are markedly behind in reading by this age generally do not catch up. On the contrary, the deficit in reading age tends to widen as they get older. Progress in other areas dependent on an adequate level of literacy is equally affected.

In light of this, a wholly unexpected finding was the number of children who learned to read 'late', even as late as 10 or 11 years of age. Even more surprising was that starting to read late had, as far as could be ascertained, no adverse effect on intellectual development, self-worth, or even subsequent attainment in literacy. In general these 'late' readers soon caught up with and passed the reading level commensurate with their ages and, in common with most other home educated children, went on to thoroughly enjoy reading.

Finding children who were apparently behind in learning to read was contrary to my own expectations that home educated children would be ahead, simply by virtue of extra individual attention. In the final analysis of 100 families, a total of 19 children (12 male, seven female) could be described as 'late' readers out of 105 who had never been to school and were aged at least 8 years of age at the time of interview. It is fair to conclude that learning to read 'late' is a feature of home education, at least for those children who have never been to school.

A finding as significant as this must be taken seriously. Parents might well exaggerate their children's attainments but are highly unlikely to dwell on what others might see as their failings. In fact, many had to field strong criticisms from spouses, relatives and friends because their children were not reading by the 'appropriate' age.

Parents expressed differing views about learning to read late.

> I find it incomprehensible that some homeschool parents can wait till their children are 9 or so. [2]

> If she is 10 and [still] hasn't learned to read we'll make a noise. [97]

Parents were naturally influenced by the usual expectations regarding reading and some were worried if their children were not reading by age 7.

> She wasn't bothered about it and it was the same with writing [but] I don't have the commitment to let her just come to things on her own. [Home education] has remained a continuation but literacy is different and I was a bit worried about it. She didn't start to read until she was 9. She's reading a lot now, Famous Five books at the moment. [77]

> [One of my sons] was $8\frac{1}{2}$ to 9 before he learned. He put up with his reading time but he was never keen. I was concerned that he had a learning impairment. At that time the Mr. Men books came out and he enjoyed them. He knew them by heart. One day we were in the car; he wanted them read. I said 'I can't read them while I'm driving. Read them yourself.' He did, correlating the written words with what he knew of the stories. From then on he read fluently. His leap was sudden if late ... I think he had no great enthusiasm and had no purpose for reading while we could read him stories. When he started, he caught up and passed his age level very quickly. I plodded with [my daughter] very slowly. The moment came when she was 10. Then she built up speed like a train on a downhill run ... She's covered a lot of ground over the last 18 months. She's reading *Lord of the Rings* at the moment. Not bad for a 12-year-old. [31]

> [My 9-year-old] has just clicked with reading. I thought he had learning problems. I had his eyes checked twice. I've now realized the problem was that I wanted him to read too much. I used phonics but it just didn't click. Now, I've just taken the pressure off ... He's very sharp and on the ball but not into reading. He's more into maths. [28]

> [She] clicked at 9. The only reading she'd done were stories we'd written out. I gave her a little book. I said 'you'll be able to read this'. She read the book and since then has never stopped. [37]

> We had a problem with reading. We thought up to age 7 or so it didn't matter ... Then we got a bit anxious. I read to her a great deal. Then at 8 she had a friend who was older who she played with a lot and who could read very well. She felt out of it. We continued to offer but she still didn't get it or wasn't motivated. Now she's very good. She's now slightly above average as a reader. [Having recently started school at 10] she is banded in the top 25 per cent. [74]

> Sometimes it's difficult to stand back. For example, she [aged 7 years] can't read ... [My partner] finds it more difficult to stand back perhaps because he is a teacher ... She likes books and will ask for them to be read to her time and again. [70]

Some came to believe that pushing children to learn to read might be a mistake if they were not receptive. There was a realization that insistence might lead to disliking an activity which should be enjoyable, both in learning and as a means for reading for oneself later on.

> We pushed him too early – a mistake on our part. He's good now. [22]

> She's not interested in reading. She only wants to read so that she can read songs for the piano. She's not reading yet; she's 7 plus. [Her brother] was reading books by then. I'm not fussed; she'll catch up. [43]

> It's often better to wait if it's going to be an effort now. The worst thing is not to enjoy learning. [44]

> [She] did not read at 6; then suddenly she showed an interest; now at 9 she is reading for herself. Two years ago she was not interested; a year ago she became motivated to find out more about reading. She doesn't read fluently yet but she's in the process of becoming fluent. But there's no pressure or force. [Her older brother] learned a lot earlier, at 5 or 6. [18]

Some learned not to pressure their younger children after having experienced difficulties with older ones.

Our eldest ... wasn't really reading before 9 years old. The learning process for reading was laborious, putting both sides through so much stress that we won't do that to the other two. [38]

When he was younger, before he went to school, I tried to teach him to read. With [his younger brother] I don't. I only read when he asks me. I would like him to enjoy books and words and time with me. I think with hindsight [my older one] felt pressure, at least sometimes, that to learn to read was, perhaps, more important than the enjoyment gained from books and time with me, and for this I feel sorry. [92]

One parent was aware of the pressure late-reading children would experience in school.

The girls read at 3. The boys wanted to play more outdoor. They were just as capable but their interests were different. They could read by 6, but not fluently. [My youngest son] was not fully reading until 9. Now he'll sit down and read a book quite happily. I'm glad he was at home because he wasn't interested in reading till last year. He's more into maths and science. [41]

The experience of these late-reading children challenges the general belief that children should learn to read by the age of 7. As mentioned above, there is good reason for it in school because of the likelihood of falling behind and the accompanying sense of failure. But why do children need to read by 7 years of age? It is simply because it is the way that teaching is organized in school. From the age of 7, most classroom tasks and activities depend heavily on reading and writing. There is, however, no theoretical rationale for it.

Disciples of the Steiner philosophy might claim that the lack of desire on the part of some children to learn to read before the age of 7 is in accord with their practice of not starting teaching of reading before this age. But there is no basis for this claim either. Many children happily learn to read before this age, sometimes without being directly taught.

Children in school who fail to learn by the prescribed age of 7 face pressure from parents and teachers alike, and possibly rejection by other children because they stand out as in need of special help. Perhaps it is because of the sense of failure on the part of the school that it is easier to locate the 'problem' in the child, ascribing lack of reading progress to various conditions such as dyslexia, attention deficit disorder, information processing disorders and various other learning difficulties, thereby inflating the actual prevalence of these conditions in the school population.

A more general and insidious consequence of the intense preoccupation with the teaching of reading in school is that many children resignedly and painstakingly acquire the mechanics of reading without enjoyment, and so never come to see it as a pleasurable activity.

Why don't these home educated children learn to read at an earlier age? Lack of interest and motivation, interest in other things, finding it difficult or boring. Perhaps it is simply because reading does not have any immediate relevance for them. If, for example, they are interested in maths, drawing and making things, playing and chatting with members of the family, there may be no need to learn to read, especially if parents are on hand to read all the stories they want and to answer all their questions. Whatever the reason, literacy does not have the urgency at home that it does in school, at least not for the children.

> He [aged 7+] can decipher a few words but he doesn't have any interest in reading ... He doesn't see it as a handicap. This is a problem for all parents. But whose problem is it? I read early. I was interested in it and loved it. It's not his problem. [85]

What these home educated children are telling us is that the age at which they learn to read, within certain limits, may not matter. As long as children have the necessary pre-reading information processing skills, and these are crucial, we should not be too concerned about when they start reading. The trouble is that this does not fit in with school organizational requirements. But the cost, in school, may be more reading failures than necessary and certainly a lessening in the enjoyment of reading as children grow older.

To sum up, being 'late' in learning to read does not, as would be expected, appear to retard general intellectual progress, affect self-esteem or detract from eventual enjoyment of reading. This parent, who gave considerable thought to her son's late start in reading, encapsulates many of the points made above.

> [He] learned to read quite late. Had he gone to school he would have experienced a lot of pressure to learn earlier. (I did not read until secondary school.) He was making progress and doing constructive things which all pointed toward literacy. It would have been negative for him in a school situation because the written word is one of their main mediums of instruction. At home we were free to continue with oral methods. He knew about letters and symbols when he was 3 or 4. But as for reading text, to be honest he was not really interested. He always had his nose in a book, though when he was younger it was visual rather than textual. He thoroughly enjoyed being read to and still does. I have not taught him. He has learned at his own pace. I hated Ladybird books, but a friend bought him one. Because he enjoyed it so much I bought him more from the series. It was right for him. We would play a game. I'd get stuck on words and he would help me. It was very much a fun thing. He is not into heavyweight novels but now his reading is fluent. He reads Famous Five books, etc. There has always been enjoyment in his reading.
>
> With home ed. children, they can always learn in a way that is appropriate to them. In school the medium is reading/writing. Children less gifted in these skills are immediately handicapped.
>
> For a long time I have answered a Home Ed Helpline. Many families who used the line had children who do not like reading and writing. At home there's more scope to communicate orally/verbally. You cannot do that with a class but you can in a family situation ...
>
> At one time my parents told [him] repeatedly that he could not read. (What they meant was he could not read as well as they expected him to.) I asked them not to say this because it was not constructive and [he] was beginning to believe them. I worked hard to rebuild his confidence.
>
> I remember when I was in school, panicking about reading aloud in class. The last thing I wanted was anything of this nature for [him]. [59]

READING FOR ENJOYMENT

Teachers are always urging children to read for enjoyment, presumably in order to improve literacy and general knowledge. But their exhortations often fall on deaf ears. Two older children, who had recently started school, remarked on their classmates' lack of interest, even ability in reading. One, aged 13, at a highly selective school said 'a lot of my friends don't like reading' [75]. The other, aged 17, in a secondary college preparing for university entrance, remarked: 'Children who don't read widely make mistakes in reading in class – all the time – it's really bad' [39]. This is commonplace, of course. University students have literacy problems!

The reason that many children in school do not read for pleasure might be that they simply do not have the time. There is very little opportunity during the school day and not a great deal of incentive to read at home after a full day in school, especially if there is homework and other after-school activities. Home educated children do have the time. And do they read!

The following is nothing less than a celebration of literacy. Let some of the parents (and a few of the children) speak for themselves.

[He] didn't read much at school. At home his reading has improved out of sight. He chooses to read non-fiction on all sorts of subjects, although he's into a Biggles phase now. [His sister's] reading is very broad, fiction and nonfiction. She's an absolutely voracious reader. When she was younger she used to read the encyclopedias. [The other sister] is more discriminating, reading authors she likes, exploring certain ideas. She reads mostly fiction. [The youngest] is reading but isn't as fluent as the girls were. But he does read and he loves his books ... Reading is something that they just do. [3]

[Daughter, 14] My interests are horses, reading fiction – adventure, and about animals in general, bushwalking; I've been reading gipsy books recently. But it's mainly horsy books.
[Mother] She's also reading *Pride and Prejudice*, Herriot and Durrell. She reads 20 to 30 books a month.
[Son, 15] I read a book every two or three days. I like James Herriot, some of [my sister's] horsy books, basically any books that look interesting. [5]

They both read and read and read ... When we go to the library they read very early books. They read every morning in bed. [6]

All the kids are voracious readers. [One] reads every day, a book a day if he's really engrossed. Sometimes he's reading two or three books at the same time. [8]

They all read for pleasure. [10]

He reads just anything. He's been reading about Leonardo da Vinci and *Jungle Story* and a novel about Cub Scouts. He likes books on dinosaurs. [12]

[Girl, 9] I like Enid Blyton books. I've read two or three of them and *Charlie and the Chocolate Factory*. Now I'm trying to get more adventure books from the library. I read most evenings and most nights. [14]

The older ones read heaps ... They are now highly critical of what they read. They can pick out prejudices in what they read. I'm amazed how they pick things out, including hidden meanings in articles. Critical thinking develops from the interaction with us. The boys don't like fiction unrelated to reality. Good fiction which is reality based is OK. They mostly read journals, e.g. on electronics – this might mirror the parents who also read non-fiction. [18]

She spends hours on the sofa reading. When she's been there too long I get her to go out. She reads all kinds of things. [24]

He is always reading. [25]

[She] had started poorly at primary school and became average. We read to her and encouraged her to read and she became voracious. She used to get a book a day from the library ... Her reading has opened up things for her. She's now interested in archaeology and history. The [other] children also enjoy the challenge of reading beyond their level. We read Shakespearean plays, each taking a different role and most days say Lauds from the

Divine Office. Although they inevitably stumble on some words, we don't worry. This gives them confidence to tackle harder things. [26]

[Girl, 13] I like horror and mystery, murder and fantasy detective – Sherlock Holmes – comedy. Sometimes I stop up until midnight reading. [27]

She could read when she came out of school, but not willingly. She needed the pressure off. I read a lot to them. Now, at 12 she reads adult history books. [28]

[Girl, 10] I like reading mysteries and spooky stories. I read as much as Mum. [29]

[She] was so fast picking up reading. She now gets twelve books a week out of the library. She consumes, eats books. It's just in, in, in. Right now it's Enid Blyton every night. She reads anything she gets her hands on. She can now research her own work. She can decide 'I'll do a project on this ... ' and get on with it herself. [33]

When they start reading you can't get them out of the bedroom. [37]

Our eldest now reads well and we have to enforce special times, otherwise she would read almost all day! She enjoys history and ancient civilizations. [38]

There is structure from 9 to 11 a.m. ... Outside this time they read a lot of novels and books. The four of them have a love of books. [41]

With reading, they love Enid Blyton and mystery stories. I lie down and read with them every night for a while. They all love books and so do I. [42]

[He] is an excellent speller and reads novels all the time, poetry, etc. [His brother] learned to read [before coming out of] school. He is an avid reader. [43]

The children all read avidly. We read as a family. [44]

As soon as he wakes up the light is on and he's in a book. [45]

We use the library but he's got heaps of books. He's just read *Myths and Legends*, 250 pages in a couple of days. He'll read anything, fiction and non-fiction. We have a neighbour of 83. She thinks he can do no wrong. He'll read her 60 pages. She really listens. [48]

He reads a lot. He's reading the Bible through for the second time. It was his own idea too. He's read the autobiography of May Gibbs. At the moment he's reading the Narnia books by C. S. Lewis. [49]

[He] reads voraciously. As a family we'd read our lives away. [51]

They might read ten books in a day. We had tons of books. We went to the library book sales – books at 50 cents each. [54]

[Boy, 14] I am trying to cut down on my reading. When I was younger I went through all the Enid Blyton books. I've recently been reading *Lord of the Flies*. I have to be careful of not reading too many very long books which you just can't put down once you've started them.
[Sister, 12] I read anything I can get from the library. I read all there is to read in one library and then have to go to another one ... the libraries all have different books to read so I have to move around. [56]

She reads profusely; she's always been an avid reader. She's always got her nose in a book. It can sometimes be rather antisocial behaviour. A year ago, on a visit to friends she'd often pick up a book to read when she's supposed to be playing. She's not quite this 'bad' now, though. [57]

He reads about two or three books a week. [62]

Both children read and read and read. [63]

She reads four or five books a week. She doesn't sleep a lot and reads instead. Now that [her brother] has discovered reading there are very long periods of quiet. [He] has read one Famous Five book and is now reading another. [69]

[She] has read tremendously. At 9 she got fed up with children's books and read all Shakespeare. She read all the plays. I read adult books I was interested in to her. It was good to stretch language. She has a compulsion to read. [Her sister] is more arty. [75]

He reads all sorts. He's read all Tintin and Asterix. He loves tales – Celtic fairy tales. I have to stop him. He reads while he's eating. He's read *Lord of the Rings* three times, the first time with his Dad, then all by himself. He's also reading the Enid Blyton Famous Five books. Also the kids' version of *The Pilgrim's Progress*. He's aware that it's an inner journey. He also reads factual books – chemistry ... He's read all Roald Dahl and Dick King-Smith. We have up to 30 library books out at any one time. [100]

She now reads anything and everything and it is more a question of 'put that book down'. [78]

[The boys] now read tremendously, including technical material, e.g. [the older one aged 9] is reading AppleMac computer magazines, *Which? Reports* and specifications of aircraft. Asked at the Steiner what they liked reading, he said: 'I like the *Chambers Concise Encyclopedia of Science.*' [His younger brother] reads a lot of Asterix stories. We go into the Classical allusions. They don't yet appreciate satire. During the day we might go to the library. When we get there they just sit down and read and read and read. [79]

She reads mainly fiction, Anastasia books. She reads a lot for pleasure, a lot of poetry, mainly at night. [80]

They are all very keen readers. They have masses of books including reference books. The older two read anything ... They all read for pleasure, but so do we. [My daughter] likes Roald Dahl and Enid Blyton and books about horses or any animals. She has just finished Dickens' *Great Expectations*. [91]

They are all competent and voracious readers. [96]

Not all home educated children are enthusiastic readers, of course. Nor is it necessary to be one to make excellent academic progress.

She is not a big reader, but she does read books for herself. [35]

Neither of the older boys were prolific readers but they are very capable and doing very well academically. [31]

Why do home educated children read so much? As suggested above, it is partly simply having the time. As we have seen, they do not spend as much time on academic work as their peers in school. They do not use up time associated with going to and coming home from school. There is no homework. Arguably they read because they would otherwise be bored. Whatever the reason there is little doubt that they enjoy reading a great deal, presumably extending their vocabulary, expression and general knowledge at the same time.

SUMMARY

In general, parents were pragmatic in their approaches to teaching reading, utilizing what seemed to work best with each child, often differing among children in the same family.

The finding that some children do not learn to read until they are between 8 and 10 years old without experiencing any adverse effect, challenges the almost general belief that it is essential for children to learn to read by the age of 7. Although most of the parents of the 'late' readers were understandably worried, their children were not. The drop in self-esteem and feeling of failure which inevitably accompany an inability to read by the appropriate time in school were not evident at home. One is left wondering just how much current educational policy, with its urgent emphasis on teaching children basic literacy by the age of 7, might actually put some children off reading, inadvertently contributing to inadequate levels of functional literacy later, or at least dampen any interest in reading for pleasure, something which home educated children certainly have, irrespective of the age they learned to read.

Chapter 10

Social Aspects

SOCIAL DEVELOPMENT

The bulk of this book is devoted to intellectual growth, but social development is equally important. The ability of children to relate socially to other children and adults plays a large part in determining personal well-being and healthy emotional development. Later on in life, adequate social skills are essential for participation in the adult world of work and leisure and for establishing and maintaining close and fulfilling relationships. As is the case with academic learning, the study of home educated children allows us, for the first time, to view social development from a very different standpoint, one which leads to reappraising certain aspects of social development in school.

As a species, we are first and foremost social beings. From the moment a child is born (even before) there is a premium on social interaction, an almost innate desire to communicate. We treat almost every sound and movement the newborn infant makes as a prompt to respond socially. This pressing preoccupation with social communication makes sound sense because it is essential for nearly everything human, including language learning and intellectual development. Social interaction is also indispensable for the formation of a secure attachment to a parent or carer in infancy, in turn essential for normal social and emotional development (Ainsworth, 1989). As children grow, their social horizons widen. Later in infancy, children start interacting with other children and making friends, which they continue to do after starting school.

It is probably because children place so much emphasis on the friends they make in school that educators and parents alike have come to assume this to be an essential benefit of schooling. School is where peer friendships flower and where children acquire the social skills necessary for survival in the real world. Or so it is believed.

In the light of this belief it is understandable that the main criticism faced by home educators does not so much concern academic progress or whether parents have the knowledge and ability to educate their children at home. Rather, it is the lack of social contact. There is a belief that if children do not go to school they will be deprived of friends, be isolated, and miss the opportunity to acquire the social skills necessary for survival in the outside world and in the workplace. They will be in danger of becoming social misfits.

In comparison with the sheer amount of contact with same-age peers in school, there is no doubt that home educated children are at a disadvantage, simply because there are few of them and because much of each day is spent at home. For those living in rural areas the problem may be more acute, though to my knowledge, no one has suggested that children brought up on isolated homesteads in the Australian outback suffer socially as a consequence.

Researching the social dimension of home education is difficult, if only because home educated children, certainly in this study, comprise a very heterogeneous group. They include children who have never been to school and those taken out of school at various stages of their school career, including some still suffering from the social distress which brought about their withdrawal from school.

Very little research has been directed at social development. What there is generally shows that home educated children are better socially adjusted (see Lines, 1995). However, no account was taken of heterogeneity. Nor were children matched with those in school on social values or other relevant variables. Still, it may be fair to conclude that being home educated is at least not socially disadvantageous. There is no evidence that home educated children experience any difficulty when they start or return to school or enter the workforce. Nevertheless, it has to be acknowledged that little is known about the long-term effects of being home educated on social develop-ment, as some parents acknowledged.

> At the back of your mind all the time is: Will they be all right? Will they be accepted in society? [85]

> You realize you are making someone different. It's a rarefied life. There's always the feeling he might find life more difficult as a result. But I have always tried to explain this to him. [95]

Mostly, after some initial misgivings, parents appeared satisfied with their children's social contacts and development, apart from some of the children who were withdrawn from school and missed the friends they had made there – prompting a few to return to school.

Many parents, as they became confident that their children were developing norm-ally, began to examine social development in school more closely. They pointed to what they saw as the negative aspects of the social culture of the school, including conformity to peer pressure, exposure to substance abuse and bullying. Some remarked that the way in which schools are organized actually promotes much of this, fostering the creation of a playground culture and virtually restricting social contact to children of the same age. Even more important might be the lack of social contact with an adult during the greater part of the day.

Making up for the lack of social contact

Parents were acutely aware of the importance of social contact and went to great lengths to compensate for the lack of it. One family had even moved house to be near other home educators.

This is the one thing they lack and we have to work on it, to find ways of giving them the company of other children. [93]

The criticism we get from friends is that there is no social contact with other kids. I try desperately to make sure they do. [2]

I bought this block because it was a good place for children to play and there were other home educators next door. [24]

I've made the effort to get them to mix with all kinds of children. They play with neighbours' kids. [68]

Because they are at home you seek out things like group activities, Cubs, etc. [89]

The most obvious source of social contact is with others who are home educated, though until quite recently such families were very few and far between. One parent, who had been home educating since the late 1970s, said how isolating it was when she started out, but that now there was a home educating community with 'as many activities as you want'. In fact, there now exist many flourishing groups of home educating families who meet on a regular basis. But the stage has not been reached where they are dotted around the neighbourhood, though a few remarked that they often bumped into other home educating families in the street or the supermarket.

We had trouble at the start because [she] was the only one for ages. Now they're everywhere; you meet them when shopping or having a day off. [39]

Most tried to make up for the lack of social contact through after-school activities, going to home education group gatherings and meeting up with other home educating families.

[He] has two main friends of 10/11 years. They are home educators who live up the road ... He's friendly with some younger children too. He's good with little kids. I'd find it hard if he didn't see someone else. [49]

When she was out [of school] I made sure that she had a lot of same-age friends. We went out a lot when she was out of school, took part in a lot of EO activities. [74]

The Home Schooling group is good. It meets once a week. [4]

They'll see other home educating kids on two or three days of the week, normally. [23]

Social contact with others is important – she gets it through Home Ed friends. I think she's missing drama with other kids – she's going to go to a very good after-school theatre school – I will keep an eye on it. [77]

They go to a lot of EO gatherings which she likes because of the social life, for example, ice skating, swimming, park and The Otherwise Club. [78]

I'm lucky because I have a lot of contact with other home educating families. Once a week or so we have visitors, but we have such a full life we don't have enough time for more ... We go on lots of excursions – off for the day, often with other home ed. families. Every second Wednesday there's the network. There were 60 children last Wednesday. Often it's just sport in summer; in winter it's craft. This term it's first aid and safety. They also have a nice social time. There is a big football oval they use. There's a playground and a beach at lunchtime or after the activities finish if they still have energy. [11]

Not all families had easy access to other home educators, not even in London or its environs where these two families lived.

The friends he had are now in school. We could easily have them around but it needs a lot of driving. There are very few doing EO – you don't have people next door doing it ... He did have home ed. friends here but not now. That exposure is missing, although in his mind he's OK. I ask him if he's lonely – 'No, I'm fine'. He never gets bored. But he does like to be with other people ... Perhaps what's lacking is the community aspect because there aren't enough people doing it. [100]

The children did not seem to find it that easy to make friends because EOers do not live near. We wondered for a time if she should go to school. [65]

The limitation of interacting only with home educating families was mentioned.

I still get doubts because home educated children only tend to mix with other home ed. children. [90]

... a thought shared by an 11-year-old boy who had recently been taken out of school.

I haven't got any home ed. friends. They're a bit strange, I find. [51]

... and by one parent.

I'm not comfortable with [other] home edders. [52]

Meeting children after school was fairly common.

After school they play with kids in the neighbourhood. A lot of peer group mixing is with school kids after school. [2]

[His] best friends both go to school. [4]

He goes out with friends after school ... His friends are jealous. He tells his friends what he's doing. Generally they say: 'You lucky sod you'. [88]

She has friends in school and a couple of them come around. We built on friendships from when she was very young. [16]

They have friends in and out of school. [10]

They have friends at all the local schools, Catholic ... State and Private, but they don't have very, very close friends. [28]

He gets on well with children in school. His friends are the same age [10] and up to 15. [53]

They both have school friends – only one in EO. [69]

They always have friends around, school friends after school. Their social life is not lacking, but Brownies is the only time they are in a large group. At the start of Brownies they were quite shy. [83]

He has too much social life. Children are always ringing the bell after school ... [99]

They play with the neighbours' children – cricket and basketball – the children are all ages. [47]

Children who had experienced social difficulties in school could find their social life improving after being taken out, even with other children in school.

[She] has more friends now than she ever had at school. She was very lonely in school. She has a friend who calls nearly every day after school. [98]

He's always had mates around within calling distance, more friends than he ever had at school. They think he does what he likes. He sees them a few times a week. We work most days till about 2, then down to the creek. He takes his bike. After that he reads. Then his friends come home from school and he's straight on the phone! [48]

Mixing with people of all ages

As most parents saw their children developing normally, they became less anxious about reduced social contact with same-age peers, claiming there were greater opportunities for more all round social development with children and adults of all ages.

> [He] has friends of all ages, including a lady in her 80s, so it is fairly varied. [59]

> They mix with young and old. The beauty of home ed. is they are allowed to play with girls too! This was taboo at school. [25]

> She enjoys the company of people of all ages – she can adapt across the whole age spectrum. [69]

> The children mix well with other children and age doesn't seem to matter. [28]

> They talk to all age groups all the time. They talk differently to different ages. [47]

> They get on well with people of whatever age. [61]

> They are quite happy to talk to adults. They are used to grown ups around. [93]

> He's developed so much self-confidence with adults. [4]

Whether or not home educated children mix more with people of all ages is open to question, though they certainly have more adult contact. Apart from the time they spend with their parents, they also meet and mix with parents of other children at home education gatherings, outings, etc. Perhaps this is partly what leads parents to believe their children are more at ease with people of all ages. In addition, they are not restricted anything as much to same-age contacts as are children in school, as some parents noted.

> They interact with people of all ages. Students in High School don't talk much to others not of the same age. [41]

> They've all got friends of different ages and play with littler ones and bigger ones. There's no age barrier at all. [34]

> Most children speak to their own age groups. Home schooled children will speak to older people and little babies. [96]

Whether or not home education is socially advantageous, it is certainly true that home educated children do have greater opportunity for certain socially enriching experiences which children in school do not.

> When [my husband's] mum was dying, they spent a lot of time with her that week. They couldn't have in school, but that was learning about real life ... When my sister had a new baby [my daughter] went to stay with her for six to eight weeks without having to pull her out of school. [3]

> When the grandparents come the children are here all the time. [8]

> [She] went [away] for a week to visit a sister who was having a baby. There was all the experience of bussing down and back and of being with someone having a baby. [10]

Social precocity

In marked contrast to the fear that children will not learn social skills if they are not in school, a number of parents remarked on their children's high level of self-assurance in dealing with adults.

They learn to relate to adults more, to look them in the face as equals. [She] argues now and then with other adults. It's a struggle – where do you draw the line? I found it hard to explain why she couldn't argue. We were staying at a friend's house. She said 'no' to something and stuck by her guns. On the other hand she could appear quite rude, letting everyone know her views. [35]

They learn a lot talking to other people. They are freer to ask what they like. They are learning to carry on a proper conversation with anyone of any age. They are not afraid to speak up or to speak to anyone. They are more confident in what they have to say and know that what they have to say is important regardless of their age. [30]

He's never had any problems of relating to anyone of any age (but not babies). Even when he was 5 people said they were frightened of him because he talked like an adult. [99]

It's the opposite of what people usually say. They are not afraid of anyone. They treat all ages as equal ... Their self-confidence took some adults aback [who] were not used to children treating them as equals. [8]

People don't like precocious kids. They want you to fit into your age group. [10]

He was in a play and he played the spirit of an autistic boy. The lady who produced it was very creative and artistic. But she had an incredible row with him. She got cross with him. He responded and he didn't back down when she said 'I'm not going to be spoken to like this'. She asked me how I'd react if it were her [the producer's] child who answered back. I said he's his own person. [90]

The following mother, who was a teacher and who had taken one of her four children out of school for a year, was torn between criticism and approval.

There was a family of home ed. people locally. They put us off. The children were very bright but socially inept. They acted like little adults rather than children – not in a way I'd expect children to act. They weren't inept with adults but couldn't fit in with same-age children from school. They put me off home education. But they were the only ones. Since, we've met others. It varies so much. We have a get together with home ed. children once a month. The children in school are very much into 'in clothes'. Home ed. children dress as they want to be dressed. They are more influenced by their mothers. There is no peer pressure. There is very little other difference that I've noticed. Home ed. kids are more polite, not rough, more open. [9]

Comparing social development at home and in school

The opportunity to develop and practise social skills in school is quite limited. Children spend nearly all their time in school with other children born during the same academic year as themselves, and a great deal of time outside school as well. In school, there is little social contact with younger or older children and even less with adults. It is easy to see how peer mores, values and codes of behaviour become entrenched, resulting in considerable pressure to conform and the threat of ostracism or exclusion from the group for those who do not. Moreover, up to one and a half hours a day in school is specifically set aside for social recreation in the playground, where children are thrown together with nothing much to do. It is not surprising that playground hierarchies emerge and bullying is rife.

The consequence is that the 'social' skills acquired are those which may be essential for survival in school but have little applicability in the outside world. There is virtually no opportunity to relate socially to adults in school in order to learn wider social skills. Ironically, such skills can only be learned outside school hours. Teachers do, of course, set up social scenarios and discuss with children how to behave in given social circumstances. But these are no substitute for learning through real-life, dynamic social contact.

Some parents were quite forthright in their views about what they believed to be the inadequacies of social experiences in school.

School doesn't reflect adult life, or how to survive in the adult situation. It trains children to survive the social complexities of an institution. While we had children in school I was frequently in a position to observe from the inside, working in the canteen, helping in the library, parent help in infant classes, taking cooking groups, supervising sports teams in High School, relief teaching and as a High School teacher before I had children ... It's becoming increasingly obvious to me that aggressive playground-style conflict resolution is not natural to children but is learned in the institutional setting. Children educated at home generally seem to bypass that stage. Instead they learn adult-type conflict resolution skills, a more suitable preparation for adulthood. [21]

It's a much more 'wholesome way' of educating. School is narrow, it's so removed from life. Others put it the other way round. [100]

Social life at school is artificial and harmful – many adults had their self-esteem crushed in school, maybe not in the early primary school but in the upper primary and High School. [16]

Peer pressure can be a strong and negative force at school. [23]

[At the school] You could see bullies picking on little ones. Kids were learning survival. The teachers said that was good – that's learning to survive. If we force kids into the playground culture, they learn to swop it for the real world. [27]

I was so brainwashed. I thought that school was where they make friends. I now realize these things are not necessarily positive and they need parental contact. [57]

One parent [at the school my two children attend one day a week] said kids should learn to settle things by fighting. They have never fought. They would take off for home. [6]

They are in a social environment at home, but not in school. In school it is enforced, and with one's peer group. There is nothing like a normal social relationship between teacher and pupil. [79]

Many parents seem to accept that their children's behaviour changes, not always positively, when they go to school, and think it is OK and normal. We question this ourselves. [45]

It's a myth children have to meet lots of other children to socialize. At school they only learn social skills they need in school because afterwards you don't mix only with people exactly your age. [20]

Home Ed is ... relaxed and there's no peer pressure to conform. This pressure of the group is the worst aspect of school. The pressure at school doesn't allow you to be yourself. [41]

I have seen many children who go to school who won't even associate with their siblings in public – who are embarrassed with them – for fear of ridicule. [26]

In school, children are blackmailed by others to make them conform ... [62]

They have friends who go to school – there is such a difference in behaviour, attitudes, respect, care and concern for each other, language, methods of play and capability of keeping themselves motivated and occupied. [28]

Children seem to change when they go to school. They are not the same. It's peer pressure, etc. You see the difference. [17]

There was a belief that ageism might owe a lot to the social milieu of the school.

> At school you start to believe it's natural and normal to be with your own age group. [92]

> In school it's the mix of too few adults with too many children. Then they only learn from their peers. [95]

> The problem that youth has with age is created by society, because we are separated from other age groups. We try artificially to bridge the gap, but at the same time we go to great lengths to create it. [18]

> A lot of children in school communicate less with adults. His friends [in school] virtually ignore me [but] he'll chat with adults ... [87]

Coming out of school and missing friends

Children who had never been to school were naturally curious about school and some were interested in going to school at some stage, but they did not express any wish to go to school for the social life. Children taken out of school, on the other hand, often did miss their friends.

> He missed school to start with. We had a lot of teething troubles, up to the summer holidays, for the first term and a half. There were tearful moments. He missed his friends. We tried to keep friendships up, but it didn't work. This is the one thing they lack and we have to work on it, to find ways of giving them the company of other children. [93]

> For [her] it's been the biggest change because she's been at school where she had a group of friends. For the first six months she said 'I'm only giving this a go you know' – since then she's got used to it. Now it's not a problem. School is not a topic any more. [37]

> She really liked home ed. last year though perhaps it's a bit lonely. [42]

> It was the one thing we felt was missing from home education. He liked to be with other children. But it's not everything. [94]

> [Daughter] I miss the friends I made in school. I had one friend – I haven't seen her since school which is a pity. [4]

> [Daughter] When I came out of school (at 11) it was completely different. It took me a long time to adjust. I'd had a few friends at school ... [26]

The decision to return to school was sometimes influenced by a lack of friends.

> It was her choice to return to school even though I felt it was too soon. I think peer pressure played a part in her return. [58]

> He didn't like being at home. He was so used to the system. I wouldn't bring him out again. [13]

> He was bored at home because there was no one his own age to play with. It was social. That's why I sent him back. They are both very social children. [19]

> She started back to school this term. It's not that she disliked home ed., rather she missed the 'people' around. [27]

> [Son] I've got four friends in school. They want me to go back. [36]

> He's missed the social contact. The older ones [in school] would have been fine at home and wouldn't have missed the social contact. [9]

> You can't develop social skills without access to the peer group. [40]

When she was at home she'd say she was bored in a pathetic voice and said she missed her friends in school. [83]

[He] missed his friends. His friends asked a lot about when he'd be coming back. He went back in September. He decided two days before ... He knew he had a choice. I was upset when he went back in. On the other hand I was pleased he'd be with his friends at school. [85]

Going to school

Children who chose to return to school found little difficulty in adjusting. Perhaps the parents of children who are experiencing serious problems in school should be encouraged to take them out for a time, home circumstances permitting.

He loved going back to school. [7]

He likes the social aspects of school. He liked the routine. He said once that he achieves more at home but he prefers to be at school. [13]

There are not too many problems. She had an excellent teacher when she went back ... When she went back she hadn't lost out. She was not behind at all. She had kept up ... She benefited from the time out of school. She certainly needed that time. She'd been throwing 2-year-old tantrums. If anything similar happened, something pretty major, we'd do it again. [46]

Her teacher was very impressed with her and thought she was lovely. She came in happy and cheerful, not shy like the other children. She had no fear of going to school, her only problem was performing to her own high standards. [57]

When she returned to school 1¾ years ago, they were amazed that she integrated so well. [85]

I don't know if she wants to stay in school. There was a patch during this term when she didn't want to go. She'll stay till the end of the year and then it depends on what she feels, and what the teacher's like. [83]

Even children who had little or no experience of school found the transition relatively painless.

The children have gone to school about Grade 6 or 7 ... They did very well at school, both finishing with lots of prizes and awards. [31]

They all went into the top year of First School at 8+. This was easier for them to adjust to than going to the first year of Middle School. They've adjusted really well. Obviously there are certain areas where there have been problems. They found copying off the board a difficult skill. [89]

Here are four older school students who described what it was like starting school for the first time or returning to school after a number of years at home. They do not seem to find it difficult to fit in to the school culture.

It was the best way to go. When I got there, there was a lot of catching up to do to understand school, for example that the teacher was the enemy. People said I went to school because I had to. Basically, I enjoyed it. It was my choice to go. [31]

School is very 'schooly', frustrating, so much time waiting for things to happen, waiting for someone to come, not having the right copy of things, waiting round while the teacher is helping others ... But I like school. I love the subjects I'm doing. I like interaction with teachers and other students. I like going out to the library – you can come and go. I thought

I'd be very behind. How was I going to cope with so many subjects? But it's been really easy. [39]

At school I feel more empathy with the teachers. [When you are] with adults more, you don't see adults as the enemy. When I picked up some books in school that the English teacher had dropped a boy said not to do it: 'The teacher's the enemy.' [75]

Starting back in school, I had to get used to it. I didn't want to go but I had to go. It didn't take that long. It was OK making friends. Now (in the second year) I'm even more used to it. [26]

The fear that home educated children will be socially isolated is understandable and parents take pains to ensure their children do not lack social contact. Nevertheless, their children can rarely experience as much contact with age-mates as their counterparts in school. Moreover, some children who are withdrawn from school do miss their friends.

Whether lack of contact with age-mates adversely affects social development is another question. Home educating parents certainly do not think it does. They go further, suggesting that it is social interaction in school which is unnatural, citing limitation of contact with children of the same age, lack of social contact with adults as well as with older and younger children.

So, how far does school succeed in preparing children for life in an adult world? How far does school, institutionally, through its structure and organization, contribute to ageism, peer conformity, bullying, initiation into substance abuse? With regard to children educated at home, are they socially more confident, independent and mature, as is claimed? Are they better prepared for entry into the adult world? The research related so far in this chapter may not provide any answers but in describing very different kinds of formative social experiences for children, it raises fundamental questions concerning the social development of all children.

OTHER SOCIAL ASPECTS

Reactions of family, friends and acquaintances

The climate for home education has changed during the last decade. Teachers and education officials are gradually becoming more understanding and supportive (see Chapter 4). This change is also discernible in the reactions of relatives, friends and other acquaintances. Nevertheless, adverse criticism still predominates, especially towards parents who decide to home educate from the outset. There is greater sympathy for parents whose children are in an intolerable situation in school, for example if they have been bullied or are patently not learning.

Reactions such the following could well deter potential home educators.

Relatives were aghast at the idea. There's a very strong pressure: 'What about the social life? They'll get isolated.' [5]

There was pressure from the family ... Why? ... How dare you! [27]

Everyone hopes deep down that you'll fail with the children. If they do well they say you are lucky. If not, people say it's ten hours a day wasted since they were born. As the children grow up there's a lot of resentment from friends and relatives; it causes tension with relatives. [15]

The hardest thing when she was out was telling my Mum and Dad. They didn't say anything. The initial pressure was from [my partner]. He'd had similar problems with his son. I said 'I'd really like your support!' [58]

The grandparents are very critical and think they should go to school. [78]

With mine [relations] there are no questions asked. They keep quiet because they don't agree. [86]

My parents are horrified and always have been. They are worried. [87]

My husband's mother's family were with us on New Year's Day and asked what school he was going to. I said 'Actually we've decided not to send him'. You could have heard a pin drop. There was an undercurrent of 'I sent mine; you should send yours' ... There was a strong letter from my mother-in-law. There was also a two and a half hour sermon from his sister ... All this distressed me at first. [99]

Some friends don't agree and they can't understand why – they are shocked. They ask: 'Are you a teacher?' At first I was embarrassed, but no longer. [17]

I was more or less the first one in [this town] to do home ed. I told her not to say she was a home schooler, because it always led to a long discussion – some people would be angry. [54]

There was a lot of opposition from lots of people: 'You're not qualified – you're not a teacher.' There was lots of negativity: 'You'll go mad.' [43]

When we first thought about it, I talked it over with a few people and got some really hostile reactions. I couldn't believe people could be so strong about it. [86]

You are always on the defensive. People challenge what we do but we don't challenge them. [99]

People hassled me: 'Is he learning?' 'You should take him back to school you know.' It was unfair. They didn't like me doing Home Ed. [7]

I have friends with kids at school. I have good and bad reactions from them, horrendous from some friends who give me terrible warnings and tell me I'm irresponsible and depriving them ... [90]

Some people felt threatened by home educators, as if they were implicitly being criticized for sending their own children to school.

With friends my own age, they feel that I am saying what they are doing is wrong and I am right. [12]

When I started, my friends were not very sympathetic. They frowned upon it: 'How much time do you have for yourself?' 'What about nourishing yourself?' But more recently some have changed and said that they felt threatened, as if they should be doing the same thing. [76]

Many feel threatened ... They wished they'd done it. People feel you are criticizing them. They get angry with you being different. There is a much greater acceptance from teachers. [54]

My sister is a career woman. She sees it as a criticism of what she's doing. [52]

These parents found reactions were mixed or improved over time.

There are mixed reactions from the relatives: 'You can't do that. You're not a teacher.' But some of them are encouraging when they see he's doing well. [50]

Some relatives have been good about it and some haven't. [47]

At the start it was 'What can you do better than the school?' [My parents] videoed programmes ripping schools apart and then their attitudes changed. We don't get any 'Put them back in school'. [Other] people either say 'Is it legal?' or 'That's a silly idea. They should be in school.' With one person I couldn't get it through it was legal. More recently people say 'I do admire you ... I wish I could have ... The trouble [my children] have had ...' [98]

Some reactions were very positive.

My parents are all for it. My father had spent a few weeks collecting him from school. They saw the effect on him. He was 'screwed up'. [88]

In the community no one opposes; there's a lot of support. They say I'm brave and they wish they had the courage. [36]

A lot of my friends say 'Good on you! I wish I could do it.' [47]

My Mum still has reservations, but has a better relationship with him now. My Dad said basically that what we are doing for him is the best thing we can do. Coming from him that's pretty good. [48]

One person was quite accepting of the situation in which an older sibling was withdrawn from secondary school, having been bullied, but was aghast that his mother had decided not to send his younger sister when she reached school age.

One lady said: 'How's [my elder son]', knowing he had had problems at school. She accepted he was educated at home, but said 'Oh no! You can't!' in respect to [my younger daughter who had just reached school age]. Others would say it's because there wasn't a man in my life. [90]

On being a home educating parent

Parents with children in school have relatively little day-to-day responsibility for their education. The only time to worry is if there are major problems. It is possible to follow an occupation and enjoy the accompanying status and financial benefits. Educating a child at home, on the other hand, is a full-time commitment in itself, with an immense amount of responsibility, added to which are all the usual household tasks, let alone the loss of a potential income. Even so, if there is anything that the parents underplayed it was the sheer magnitude of the task they had undertaken, but they do admit to finding it very demanding.

I found it tiring more than anything I'd ever done. They always wanted that attention. They use you to find out. [61]

I find it all very demanding and take Friday off when [my husband] takes over. [63]

I've been weary at times – I get tired – occasionally I go off for the day. [43]

It's a dynamic exercise. You need a lot of mental and emotional energy for it. [24]

It is very tiring and very difficult to find time for oneself. [64]

At the moment we are not doing that well. We can't find time easily. We [each] get a break when one of us takes the kids out. [37]

I find being an EOer exhausting. [68]

She physically drained me. [57]

I still do wonder ... It's a terrific amount of work. [77]

There are days when I tear my hair out and think I must be insane. [45]

[She] wanted more input from me which I couldn't give. I found it hard to be with her at home the whole time. [83]

But not for everyone ...

I don't find it tiring but I had three children last time within less than five years. [70]

It is not tiring, I have lots of energy. Anyway being tired is not a negative experience. [72]

I miss out on having more time for myself and being able to do things spontaneously during the day. But advantages outweigh disadvantages. [85]

It's not tiring. We go about our jobs and they come with us. [23]

Surprisingly, feeling isolated was hardly mentioned, perhaps because the task is all-consuming. A number of parents were following outside activities independently of their children, for example, part-time work, involvement with home education organizations, part-time study, helping with the family business, evening classes and so on. Parents were naturally concerned about whether they were doing the right thing.

You often feel paranoid about doing the right thing – you hear that someone else is doing fractions and you think: Oh God! I haven't even started that! [62]

I'm filled with doubts and fears. It's a big risk. [97]

If you challenge the system you feel guilty. [27]

I agonize over whether I'm doing the right thing. [12]

With time, parents tended to become more confident, as they saw their children progressing satisfactorily ...

Sometimes you feel a bit despondent and overwhelmed by the enormity of the task at hand – until you see results, look at their work and see what they've done. [26]

... or when they received positive feedback from outsiders.

I need regular positive feedback and find the lack of it difficult to cope with. When children are in school there is regular feedback. I need people to tell me that the children are doing well, or otherwise. But more recently I have become more confident, having just had positive feedback from a LEA inspection visit, the first one for 18 months. [76]

Virtually no one regretted the loss of income or status. Many parents indicated they were learning or had learned a great deal that was positive from the experience, in terms of personal development and close involvement with their children, watching them blossom intellectually and socially.

It's changed me, challenged me, otherwise I would have worked and had money. [68]

I feel as if I've done a university course. I've become very self-aware. You see yourself from the child's point of view. Oh goodness! I can't behave like this. I have explored myself a great deal through EO. [75]

My education has taken off. I know what learning is all about now. I'm not sure I did before. [77]

It's made me feel a lot stronger. I'd have bowed to people's opinions a lot more – in other things as well. [84]

While it is true we start from a place of having a belief system, it is also true that much of what I think now has developed over the years of watching and learning from my own children. I feel that I have been on a journey of discovery; I am the one who is learning all the time. [63]

I'm grateful to him. You go to work for money. Now I've got time for things I've never done before. It's me who's taken up interests from some of the things I've taught [him]. Not him! I've completely changed my view of school. [88]

My own education started when [he] came out of school. [90]

I'm not sure who gets most out of home schooling, them or me. We certainly all benefit. [45]

I'm learning with him. I truanted mostly at school, but lots of things I thought boring, he's interested in – science, history and geography. [92]

It's a real adventure, home schooling. [47]

Home education is impossible. When I talk with home educating friends we realize it's incredible what we are trying to do. But the whole idea is exciting. It requires self-awareness, self-assessment and self-examination. [24]

Funny thing about it all is that I'm learning too. I'm interested in everything. I get excited. I pick up a geology book. I'm as interested in learning as they are; that's a positive thing. [10]

We always get sidetracked while working. We do a lot of shared learning. I'm having my own primary education. [19]

Parents learn a lot. You learn about yourself. You explain what you know but it nearly always leads to things you don't know. We search for answers together. It's a co-operation to search for answers. [18]

Two parents were disappointed with their experience of home education.

I had this exciting idea about home ed. which hasn't materialized. [87]

Sometimes I try to explain why I failed at home ed. ... He's always wound me round his little finger, so no wonder it didn't work out ... He's much more friendly now he's in school. [7]

SUMMARY

Social development

Home educated children obviously have less opportunity to mix socially with other children of the same age. But this does not appear to hamper their personal or social development, or the acquisition of social skills. On the contrary, most parents came to believe their children had a more normal social upbringing than if they had been in school. They pointed out that children in school experience very little adult social contact in comparison with home educated ones. More contentiously, they criticized the narrowing effects of being part of the same-age subculture in school, with its restricted view of the world and pressure, sometimes physical, to conform to its mores. It was also pointed out how the institution of schooling directly fosters the development of such a subculture. It is reasonable to ask whether school is the best place to learn social skills other than those obviously necessary for survival in school.

Children who are withdrawn from school may, understandably, miss their friends, the reason given by some for wanting to return to school. Home educated children who start school for the first time or return to school after a period at home do not seem to experience any major difficulty in making the transition.

Other social aspects

Home education requires an enduring commitment and usually entails giving up a career with the consequent loss of status and income. Instead, parents take on the job of full-time unpaid educator, usually without training and with the responsibility. In effect, they are challenging nearly two centuries of accumulated professional wisdom, underpinned by a massive amount of research. In addition, they may have to field criticism from relatives and friends, even from people in the street.

All this is in addition to the task itself. Parents have to find out how to go about it as they go along. There are no guidelines or handbooks. They have to find and then pay for books and other educational materials. Most of all, they are then in demand all day. The task is all-consuming.

In spite of all this, parents generally come to regard what they do as a career in itself. The experience of being instrumentally and intimately involved in all aspects of their children's education is generally found to be both enriching and fulfilling.

Chapter 11

A Different Kind of Education

At the very least, the research described in this book confirms that education at home is a viable alternative to school. Parents or carers do not need any special training or qualifications. Moreover, they often educate their children with very limited resources and with little or no professional guidance. This is radical enough in itself, but it goes much further than this. As parents come to grips with the task of educating their children at home they make educational discoveries which do not reveal themselves in the classroom, some of which directly challenge received wisdom and practice.

When educational professionals visit home educators their main concern, from their perspective, is whether the parents or carers are able to provide their children with an educational experience on a par with what they would experience in school. There is an assumption, based on accumulated professional expertise, that educational methods and procedures used in school must be the yardstick against which to measure the effectiveness of home education. This is perfectly reasonable, if only because education has taken place in classrooms over such a long period of time. It is natural that home educators should intend to implement these school methods at home.

Yet, when parents embark on their task they generally find that it does not turn out as they envisaged. Standard educational methods do not transfer into the home. As the parents fashion a pedagogy suitable to their circumstances, they find themselves trying out approaches which would be impossible even to attempt in school. Their experiences provide us with new and sometimes striking insights into education and child development.

DIFFERENT APPROACHES TO TEACHING

There is a great deal of debate about whether the quality of classroom teaching and learning has improved, certainly during the second half of the twentieth century. Whatever the case, all attempts to gauge improvement are restricted because any comparisons are with other kinds of classroom teaching and learning. Up to a point this is fair enough because education is almost always a classroom activity. The drawback is that we fail to appreciate that most of the existing body of knowledge, logically, only applies to the population of classroom educated children, thereby confining our understanding of the nature of teaching and learning.

This limited perspective influences home educators too. When parents start out, the obvious path to follow is that of 'doing school' at home. With experience, however, virtually all the parents gravitate away from school methods. The approaches they eventually adopt range from relatively formal and structured through to completely informal. During the course of the research it became possible to appreciate each family's philosophy and the way it had evolved with experience. With regard to educational progress and achievement, the method used may not matter. The over-riding advantage is probably the individual attention that children get, whatever the approach.

Most people, when they try to visualize home education, tend to see it as an imitation of school, with children working at desks or the kitchen table, for the equivalent of the school day, in front of their teacher-parents who teach carefully prepared lessons which cover the school curriculum – ensuring their children are kept on task, asking questions, regularly marking their work and assessing progress. Few conform to this image.

The greater flexibility which home education allows means that a timetable is unnecessary and is usually dropped altogether. Moreover, lessons can be put off for another time if a child is obviously not learning effectively for whatever reason. Parents are able to take advantage of those times when their children are most receptive, including the evenings and weekends.

At home, lessons are concentrated and intensive. This is mainly due to extra individual attention and also because very little time is spent on the kind of peripheral activities which take up much of classroom time. In consequence, lessons are short and so is the working day, generally restricted to the morning or part of it. This is in stark contrast with the current educational fashion of more and more homework in addition to school and more and more school for children who are failing, including school in the holidays.

By far the most important difference between more formal, structured learning at home and in school, though, is that learning at home becomes an interactive process rather than a series of tasks to be tackled. Parents repeatedly refer to being able to strike while the iron's hot, to deal with problems as they arise, not going on to something new until the prerequisite knowledge or concepts have been acquired. If children get stuck they do not proceed until the problem has been dealt with. In fact, any mistakes they make, rather than creating barriers to learning, simply inform their parents of their thinking processes. Errors, therefore, simply become steps on the route to enlightenment. Because they experience little failure, children become confident in their ability to learn. This is in marked contrast with the classroom where children are constantly being graded and measured against their peers, however subtly.

A more fundamental pedagogical change occurs as parents gradually discover the potential of informal teaching and learning. There is nothing in the way children learn in school to suggest how powerful informal learning might be. Two influences impel parents toward informal styles of learning. The first is the result of their own observations. They find themselves talking a lot with their children, following through their interests, answering questions, drawing their attention to things which might arouse their curiosity, even during more formal learning sessions.

A second, possibly more potent influence, is the way in which some children resist more formal teaching. If they lose interest or do not understand, they stop listening. Because it is in a one-to-one situation, the feedback for the parent is immediate and acute. Dogged persistence is fruitless. What is the point of explaining something to someone who is patently not taking it in? Children in school who resist learning or do not pay attention must somehow be cajoled into compliance, or at least a pretence of it. There is no other option. If a child persists in not learning or attending, the fault is located in the child or his or her background. At home, on the other hand, parents begin to see that their children are not necessarily being lazy or uncooperative. They just want to learn in a different way, though they may not be able to articulate how.

CHILDREN'S IMPLICIT AND UNACKNOWLEDGED THEORY OF LEARNING

From birth, children apply themselves rigorously to becoming competent members of their culture. Most of what they learn during the early years is acquired informally, through everyday interaction with their parents/carers. There is no reason, a priori, why this optimally effective cultural apprenticeship cannot be extended through the primary school years and beyond. Nevertheless, the proposition that children might acquire an education, well into the secondary years, simply through an apprenticeship in everyday living is, on the face of it, implausible. As an idea though, it is certainly not new. Before universal schooling, most cultural knowledge was transmitted in this way. Nearer our time, George Eliot had given it some thought:

> Mary ... gave the boys little formal teaching, so that Mrs Garth was alarmed lest they should never be well grounded in grammar and geography. Nevertheless, they were found quite forward enough when they went to school; perhaps, because they had liked nothing so well as being with their mother. (Eliot, *Middlemarch*, 1872, p. 834)

Informal learning, piecemeal though it may be, somehow or other fuses into a coherent body of cultural knowledge, including acquisition of the appropriate levels of conceptual and cognitive understanding, like 'growing leaves on trees' as one parent put it [77]. Or another:

> School seems unnatural. With a huge effort and cost and sometimes pain, you try to get something into the children which would happen anyway. [18]

A small number of parents, recognizing their children had been progressing intellectually throughout the first few years of life, simply continued and extended on what they were already doing. Most others reduced formal learning; a few abandoned it altogether. By no means does this mean that learning is left to chance. Parents still have the role they have had since their children were born, of inducting them into the culture. They accomplish this by extending on what their children already know, introducing new topics and responding to their children's interests. Much of this occurs incidentally through everyday conversation which, on the surface at least, is perceived as social rather than a means to intellectual growth. Because the conversation is with an adult, the children are able to hone their thinking skills, improve their expression and increase their vocabulary and general knowledge. It is simply cultural transmission by osmosis rather than through deliberate teaching. Of course, informal learning is not restricted to childhood. Throughout life we are constantly learning informally in the context of everyday activities, at work, socially and at home, again with little awareness that we are actually learning anything.

What are the characteristics of the child's theory of learning? First, there is a general lack of awareness that any specific learning is taking place. Concepts are acquired, skills improved and new knowledge gained during the course of concrete, everyday activities or through other topics which have captured the child's interest. An activity, from the child's point of view, may be helping to make cakes, going for a walk, shopping, going out in the car, reading a book, making a house out of a cardboard box, and so on. Any learning episodes, in maths, language, science, geography or whatever, are not differentiated but are simply part and parcel of the concrete activity. They may be integral to the activity, such as maths in shopping and science in cooking, or incidental to it, occurring through social conversation during a walk, in the car or at mealtimes. Whatever the case, from the child's point of view it is the activity which is paramount. The intellectual element goes unnoticed. Learning is therefore contextualized in a way it rarely is in formal lessons.

The culture of the home obviously has to be conducive to informal learning. Parents must be actively committed guides and mentors for their children, leading them ever onwards towards becoming fully-fledged members of the culture. Not much informal learning is going to occur if children are left to their own devices. Informal learning is not licence. Parents must have, at the back of their minds, a general mental picture of what they want their children to achieve: literacy, numeracy, a good general knowledge, etc. This is their informal curriculum. Parents have a more crucial role to play than is the case with formal learning in which children do at least have graded curriculum material to work with. They have to be attuned to what their children know and what interests them. They have to be ready to introduce them to new knowledge at the right moment, when it is likely to be assimilated. What makes informal learning so difficult to pin down is that parents themselves are for the most part unaware of what their children are learning. As some parents remarked, it was only when they looked back over what they had done, or kept a careful record, that they could see how much learning had taken place.

Informal learning is obviously not ordered or sequential in the way that it is in school. A curriculum or a programme of learning would be deemed very poor indeed if it were not logically developed and graded into digestible morsels. But it does not follow that children can only learn effectively by following such carefully predetermined steps. When they learn informally, children impose their own sequence on what they learn. Curriculum logic and psychological logic do not necessarily equate. Psychological sequence is determined by the complex and dynamic interaction between the child's level of knowledge, interest, motivation, etc., and the parent's ability to dovetail her 'teaching' accordingly, depending on her intuitive appraisal of the situation. There is even an informal timetable, a psychological one, determined by the child's level of motivation, interest and conceptual preparedness. 'Lessons' occur when they are most likely to be learned, so that knowledge or understanding is most easily assimilated. If the material being processed goes beyond the child's understanding or capacity for attending, it ceases to be assimilated. The 'lesson' is over.

Informal learning is highly efficient. It must be if one is largely unaware of it happening. From an information-processing standpoint, it is only meaningful incoming

information which is processed, that which extends existing knowledge, arouses interest or curiosity, or serves to consolidate or rehearse what is already partly known. Any
incoming information which does none of these things is filtered out, discarded. These
processes are controlled metacognitively by the child. Of course there are times when
a learning opportunity will be lost. But these will be more than compensated by the
efficiency with which learning takes place when the child is attentive.

Increments in learning are extremely difficult to pin down. Fortuitously, one parent
provided a very detailed record of her child's informal learning over a number of years,
one very small part of which is described in Chapter 8, demonstrating in great detail
how it is feasible to acquire an education informally. We were able, for the first time, to
'see' actual increments in learning in maths, even though the child in question did not
really 'do' maths, certainly not in the formal sense. She helped with cooking and
shopping, went on car journeys, collected supermarket 'trolley money' and came to
appreciate the value of material goods, all of which included maths, but she did not see
it like that. She saw only the concrete activity. If she did count money on occasion, or
did 'sums' in her head, it was her decision, sparked by her emerging understanding or
simple curiosity about number. Incidentally, there is very little maths *qua* maths in
everyday life though it is an essential part of many everyday activities. The point is that
maths, certainly most of what is acquired at the primary level, can be learned as an
integral part of everyday concrete activities. In school, maths has to be divorced from
the dynamic realities of everyday life. To reiterate a point made in Chapter 8, children
in school learn maths by doing maths. This child learned most of her maths when she
was doing something else.

Informal learning is not confined to children educated at home. Children who go to
school no doubt learn a great deal informally outside school hours. It would be
interesting to know just how much academic progress charted in school might actually
be attributed to learning informally outside school when many children have the
opportunity to put their own theories of learning into practice.

As well as on teaching and learning in general, home educators offer different
perspectives on literacy. Their experiences suggest that the debate about methods of
teaching children to read may be important when it is necessary to teach a large number
of children at the same time, but is largely irrelevant when teaching is at an individual
level. Home educated children learn to read at different ages, and through a great
variety of methods, even within the same family. The finding that some children learn
to read 'late', without apparent disadvantage, leads one to question the urgency with
which schools try to get all children to read acceptably by the age of 7. It may be
necessary in school because learning from the age of 7 is heavily dependent on the
ability to read and write acceptably. The consequence of such pressure may be to
alienate many children from reading for enjoyment and from the contribution such
reading makes to the further development of literacy and general knowledge.

The initial worries which home educators have concerning social development
gradually fade as they see their children growing up, confident and relaxed in adult
company and able to relate to children of all ages. This leads some to question the
popular assumption that school is the best preparation for entry into the social world of
adults. They ask if the playground is the best place to learn social skills and why it is
supposedly beneficial to spend so much of the day with age-mates. They point to the
lack of opportunity there is in school to learn social skills from adults by actually

practising them. In consequence, some parents suggest that it is school which is cut off from the real world.

Educating a child at home is a full-time and highly demanding commitment, nearly always undertaken by the mother. In very few instances is the responsibility shared. In addition, it generally means giving up an income and a career. On top of this, many have to field criticisms from relatives and acquaintances who are sometimes quite antagonistic. Nevertheless, most parents found being fully involved in their children's education both rewarding and intellectually enriching.

The vast majority of us still live in a predominantly 'school' culture in which our attitudes to children, work, career and financial status are partly fashioned by the fact that our children go to school. A radical shift in the way children are educated would require major changes both in society and in attitudes to education which could take generations to evolve. One parent had given considerable thought to what this would mean. In particular she points to the cultural expectations most of us conform to, including the dread of having to spend holidays with our children which has almost become a cultural norm. Newspapers regularly devote articles on how to survive children during the holidays, even the weekends.

> Some parents say they are glad to wave goodbye to their children when they go to school ... true for all of us for some of the time ... I suspect that in many cases it is a matter of expectation, conditioning and attitude, i.e. it is not so unusual to be at home all day with your children and enjoy their company. More parents would be free to enjoy such if they weren't themselves the subject of so much peer pressure, materialistic demands, social norms, etc. [63]

The research in this book is exploratory; it is premature to discuss implications in any detail. With regard to children in school, educational policy might evolve gradually towards catering more for the individual child in the only practical way possible, by further encouraging the existing trend toward parental involvement and responsibility. In the longer term, more flexible approaches to schooling might evolve, such as 'flexischooling' as suggested by Meighan (1988). Home education is also likely to become more feasible with the rapid increase in the quality of interactive educational software and the worldwide access to information available through the Internet (see Hargreaves, 1997).

Over the last twenty years, education authorities and departments have moved from opposition to tolerance and, in a few instances, have provided support for home educators. Home education is gradually coming to be viewed as an appropriate rather than radical alternative to school. The next step might be to provide workshops and access to educational resources and advice. There is no reason why education authorities or departments should not receive funding for home educated children in order to offer activities and provide resources. Alternatively, home educators themselves might be funded, as they already are in New Zealand, for example.

Home educators give us a view of education which, in many respects, is markedly different from what is on offer in school. What they have learned from their pioneering experiences has the potential to bring about the most fundamental change in education since the advent of universal schooling in the nineteenth century.

References

Adams, A. K. (1987) 'A penguin belongs to the bird family': language games and the social transfer of categorical knowledge. Paper presented to the Third International Conference on Thinking, Honolulu, January.

Ainsworth, M. D. S. (1989) Attachments beyond infancy. *American Psychologist*, **34**, 932–7.

Allen, V. L. (ed.) (1976) *Children as Teachers: Theory and Research on Tutoring*. New York: Academic Press.

Anania, J. (1983) The influence of instructional conditions on student learning and achievement. *Evaluation and Education: An International Review Series*, **7**, 1–92.

Barnes, D.(1969) *Language, the Learner and the School*. Harmondsworth: Penguin.

Bendell, J. (1987) *School's Out*. Bath: Ashgrove Press.

Bennett, N. and Desforges, C. (1985) (eds) *Recent Advances in Classroom Research*. Edinburgh: Scottish Academic Press.

Bennett, N., Desforges, C., Cockburn, A. and Wilkinson, B. (1984) *The Quality of Pupil Learning Experiences*. London: Lawrence Erlbaum Associates.

Bloom, B. S. (1984) The 2-sigma problem: the search for methods of group instruction as effective as one-to-one teaching. *Educational Research* (June/July).

Bloom, B. S. (1985) *Developing Talent in Young People*. New York: Ballantine Books.

Board of Education (1927) *Handbook of Suggestions for the Consideration of Teachers*. London: HMSO.

Brown, R. and Bellugi, U. (1964) Three processes in the child's acquisition of syntax. In Lenneberg, E. H. (ed.) *New Directions in the Study of Language*. Cambridge, MA: MIT Press.

Bruner, J. S. (1983) *Child's Talk: Learning to Use Language*. Oxford: Oxford University Press.

Bruner, J. S. (1990) Foreword. In Grieve, R. and Hughes, M. (eds) *Understanding Children*. Oxford: Basil Blackwell.

Butterworth, G. and Cochran, E. (1980) What minds have in common in space: a perceptual mechanism for joint reference in infancy. *International Journal of Behavioral Development*, **3**, 253–72.

Carins, K. (1995) Home education: the Tasmanian model. *Proceedings* of the Conference of the Australasian Association of Distance Education Schools, Hobart, September.

Carraher, T. N., Carraher, D. W. and Schliemann, A. D. (1985) Mathematics in the streets and in the schools. *British Journal of Developmental Psychology*, **3**, 21–9.

Child, D. (1985) Educational psychology: past, present and future. In Entwistle, N. (ed.) *New Directions in Educational Psychology I: Learning and Teaching*. Lewes: Falmer Press.

Cobb, A. and Hagemaster, J. (1987) The criteria for evaluating qualitative research proposals. *Journal of Nursing Education*, **26**, 138–42.

Cohen, P. A., Kulik, J. A. and Kulik, C.-L. C. (1982) Educational outcomes of tutoring: a meta-analysis of findings. *American Educational Research Journal*, **19**, 237–48.

Crystal, D. (1976) *Child Language, Learning and Linguistics*. London: Edward Arnold.

Damon, W. (1984) Peer education: the untapped potential. *Journal of Applied Developmental Psychology*, **5**, 331–43.

Department of Education and Science (1980–82) *Mathematical Development*. Secondary Survey Reports, Assessment of Performance Unit. London: HMSO.

Dewey, J. (1933) *How We Think*. Boston, MA: D. C. Heath and Company.

Driver, R. (1985) Changing perspectives on science lessons. In Bennett, N. and Desforges, C. (eds) *Recent Advances in Classroom Research*. Edinburgh: Scottish Academic Press.

Dworkin, M. S. (1959) *Dewey on Education*. New York: Teachers College Press.

Education Otherwise (1993) *School Is Not Compulsory: A Guide to Home-based Education*. Badgers Holt, Birchwood, Storridge, Malvern, Worcs WR13 5HA.

Eliot, G. (1872) *Middlemarch*. London: Penguin Classics, 1994.

Ellis, S. and Rogoff, B. (1982) The strategies and efficacy of child versus adult teachers. *Child Development*, **53**, 730–5.

Feldman, D. H. with Goldsmith, L. T. (1986) Transgenerational influences in the development of early prodigious behaviour: a case study approach. In Fowler, W. (ed.) *Early Experience and Competence Development*. San Francisco: Jossey-Bass.

Fowler, W. (1990) Early stimulation and the development of verbal talents. In Howe, M. J. A. (ed.) *Encouraging the Development of Exceptional Skills and Talents*. Leicester: The British Psychological Society.

Francis, H. (1985) Reading development in school. In Bennett, N. and Desforges, C. (eds) *Recent Advances in Classroom Research*. Edinburgh: Scottish Academic Press.

Galton, M., Simon, P. and Croll, P. (1980) *Inside the Primary Classroom*. London: Routledge and Kegan Paul.

Garforth, F. W. (1966) *John Dewey: Selected Educational Writings*. London: Heinemann.

Goodlad, S. and Hirst, B. (eds) (1990) *Explorations in Peer Tutoring*. Oxford: Blackwell Education.

Hargreaves, D. H. (1997) A road to the learning society. *School Leadership and Management*, **17**, 9–21.

Harrison, D. (1988) *The Common People*. London: Penguin.

Hart, K. (1985) Mathematics education research. In Bennett, N. and Desforges, C. (eds) *Recent Advances in Classroom Research*. Edinburgh: Scottish Academic Press.

Heber, M. (1981) Instruction versus conversation as opportunities for learning. In Robinson, W. P. (ed.) *Communications in Development*. London: Academic Press.

Heyns, B. (1978) *Summer Learning and the Effects of Schooling*. New York: Academic Press.

Holmes, E. G. A. (1919) *What Is and What Might Be*. London: Constable.

Home Education Advisory Service (1996) *Information Pack*. PO Box 98, Welwyn Garden City, Herts AL8 6AN.

Howe, M. J. A. (1990) *Encouraging the Development of Exceptional Skills and Talents*. Leicester: The British Psychological Society.

Hunter, R. (1995) The home education phenomenon: paradoxes of individualization and internalization. Paper presented to the 30th Annual Meeting of the Comparative and International Education Society.

Hurt, J. S. (1979) *Elementary Schooling and the Working Classes, 1860–1918*. London: Routledge and Kegan Paul.

Joffe, L. and Foxman, D. (1989) *Communicating Mathematical Ideas*. London: HMSO.

Lawrence, E. (1970) *The Origins and Growth of Modern Education*. London: Penguin Books.

Limbrick, E., McNaughton, S. and Glynn, T. (1985) Reading gains for underachieving tutors and tutees in a cross age peer tutoring programme. *Journal of Child Psychology and Psychiatry*, **26**, 939–53.

Lines, P. (1991) Estimating the home schooled population. Working Paper. Washington, DC: US Department of Education, Office of Research and Improvement, October.

Lines, P. (1995) *Home Schooling: ERIC Digest* 95. Clearinghouse of Educational Management, University of Oregon.

Lloyd, P. (1990) Children's communication. In Grieve, R. and Hughes, M. (eds) *Understanding Children*. Oxford: Basil Blackwell.

Mayberry, M., Knowles, J. G., Ray, B. and Marlow, S. (1995) *Home Schooling*. Thousand Oaks, CA: Corwin Press Inc.

Meadows, S. (1986) *Understanding Child Development*. London: Hutchinson.

Meighan, R. (1984a) Home-based educators and education authorities: the attempt to maintain a mythology. *Educational Studies*, **10**, 273–86.

Meighan, R. (1984b) Political consciousness and home-based education. *Educational Review*, **36**, 165–73.

Meighan, R. (1988) *Flexischooling*. Ticknall, Derbyshire: Education Now Publishing Cooperative.

Meighan, R. (1995) Home-based education effectiveness research and some of its implications. *Educational Review*, **47**, 275–87.

Meighan, R. (1997) *The Next Learning System*. Nottingham: Educational Heretics Press.

Palinscar, A. S. and Brown, A. L. (1986) Interactive teaching to promote independent learning from text. *Reading Teacher*, **39**, 771–7.

Paterson, J. L. (1995) Home education in Grampian. Unpublished MEd dissertation, University of Aberdeen.

Petrie, A. (1992) Home education and the Local Education Authority. Unpublished PhD dissertation, University of Liverpool.

Petrie, A. (1993) Education at home and the law. *Education and the Law*, **5**, 139–44.

Petrie, A. (1995) Home educators and the law within Europe. *International Review of Education*, **41**, 285–96.

Petrie, A. (1998) Trends in home education (in preparation).

Plowden Report (1967) *Children and Their Primary Schools* (2 vols). Report of the Central Advisory Council for Education in England. London: HMSO.

Radziszewska, B. and Rogoff, B. (1988) Influence of adult and peer collaboration on children's planning skills. *Developmental Psychology*, **24**, 840–8.

Ray, B. D. (1997) *Strengths of Their Own: Home Schoolers Across America*. Salem, OR: National Home Education Research Institute Publications.

Ray, B. D. and Wartes, J. (1991) The academic achievement and affective development of home-schooled children. In Van Galen, J. and Pitman, M. A. (eds) *Home Schooling: Political, Historical and Pedagogical Perspectives*. Norwood, NJ: Ablex Publishing Corporation.

Reed, M. (1984) *Educating Hearing-Impaired Children*. Milton Keynes: Open University Press.

Rogers, D. (1985) Infants, mothers and intentional communication. In Branthwaite, A. and Rogers, D. (eds) *Children Growing Up*. Milton Keynes: Open University Press.

Rogoff, B. (1990) *Apprenticeship in Thinking*. New York: Oxford University Press.

Rogoff, B. and Wertsch, J. V. (1984) Children's learning in the 'zone of proximal development'. In *New Directions for Child Development*, no. 23. San Francisco: Jossey-Bass.

Rowland, S. (1984) *The Enquiring Classroom*. London: The Falmer Press.

Schaffer, H. R. (1977) *Mothering*. London: Open Books/Fontana.

Schaffer, H. R. (1984) *The Child's Entry into a Social World*. London: Academic Press.

Shaffer, D. R. (1989) *Developmental Psychology*. Pacific Grove, CA: Brooks/Cole Publishing Company.

Sharpley, A. M. and Sharpley, C. F. (1981) Peer tutoring: a review of the literature. *CORE: Collected Original Resources in Education*, **5**, 7–11.

Sheasgreen, W. J. (1986) John Locke and the charity school movement. *History of Education*, **15**, 63–79.

Smith, P. K. and Cowie, H. (1988) *Understanding Children's Development*. Oxford: Basil Blackwell.

Snow, C. E. (1977) The development of conversation between mothers and babies. *Journal of Child Language*, **4**, 1–22.

Sosniak, L. A. (1990) The tortoise, the hare, and the development of talent. In Howe, M. J. A. (ed.) *Encouraging the Development of Exceptional Skills and Talents*. Leicester: The British Psychological Society.

Taniuchi, C. (1982) The creation of prodigies. Paper presented to the Bernard van Leer Foundation, The Hague.

Tasmanian Home Education Advisory Council (1996) *Information Kit*. Education Department, Launceston, Tasmania 7250.

Thomas, A. (1992) Individualised teaching. *Oxford Review of Education*, **18**, 59–74.

Thomas, A. (1994) Conversational learning. *Oxford Review of Education*, **20**, 131–42.

Tizard, B. and Hughes, M. (1984) *Children Learning at Home and in School*. London: Fontana.

Tizard, J., Schofield, N. N. and Hewison, J. (1982) Collaboration between teachers and parents in assisting children's reading. *British Journal of Educational Psychology*, **52**, 1–15.

Topping, K. (1988) *The Peer Tutoring Handbook: Promoting Cooperative Learning*. London: Croom Helm.

Topping, K. (1992) Cooperative learning and peer tutoring: an overview. *The Psychologist: Bulletin of the British Psychological Society*, **5**, 151–61.

Van Galen, J. (1991) Ideologues and pedagogues. In Van Galen, J. and Pitman, M. A. (eds) *Home Schooling: Political, Historical and Pedagogical Perspectives*. Norwood, NJ: Ablex Publishing Corporation.

Van Galen, J. and Pitman, M. A. (1991) *Home Schooling: Political, Historical and Pedagogical Perspectives*. Norwood, NJ: Ablex Publishing Corporation.

Webb, J. (1990) *Children Learning at Home*. London: The Falmer Press.

Wells, G. (1986) *The Meaning Makers: Children Learning Language and Using Language to Learn*. London: Hodder and Stoughton.

Wertsch, J. V. and Kanner, B. G. (1992) A sociocultural approach to intellectual development. In Sternberg, R. J. and Berg, C. A. (eds) *Intellectual Development*. Cambridge, MA: Cambridge University Press.

Wilkinson, A. (1985) Writing. In Bennett, N. and Desforges, C. (eds) *Recent Advances in Classroom Research*. Edinburgh: Scottish Academic Press.

Wood, D. J. (1988) *How Children Think and Learn*. Oxford: Basil Blackwell.

Wood, D. J. (1992) Peer commentary on: K. Topping, Cooperative learning and peer tutoring: an overview. *The Psychologist*, **5**, 160.

Wood, D. J., Wood, H. A. and Middleton, D. J. (1978) An experimental evaluation of four face-to-face teaching strategies. *International Journal of Behavioral Development*, **1**, 131–47.

Index of Families

(NB: nos 1–58, Australian families; nos 59–100, UK families)

Name Index

Adams, A. K. 26
Ainsworth, M. D. S. 111
Allen, V. L. 15
Anania, J. 16

Barnes, D. 19
Bellugi, U. 23
Bendell, J. 25, 33
Bennett, N. 3, 12, 18, 84
Bloom, B. S. 4, 16, 26
Brown, A. L. 15
Brown, R. 23
Bruner, J. S. 21
Butterworth, G. 22

Carins, K. 2
Carraher, D. W. 71
Carraher, T. N. 71
Child, D. 3
Cobb, A. 8
Cochran, E. 22
Cockburn, A. 3
Cohen, P. A. 15
Cowie, H. 22, 23
Croll, P. 3
Crystal, D. 23

Damon, W. 16
Desforges, C. 3
Dewey, J. 3, 10–11, 12, 13
Driver, R. 19
Dworkin, M. S. 11

Eliot, G. 128
Ellis, S. 16

Feldman, D. H. 26
Fowler, W. 26
Foxman, D. 13
Francis, H. 17

Galton, M. 3, 12, 19, 46
Garforth, F. W. 11
Glynn, T. 15
Goldsmith, L. T. 26
Goodlad, S. 16

Hagemaster, J. 8
Hargreaves, D. H. 131
Harrison, D. 98
Hart, K. 18
Heber, M. 26
Hewison, J. 17
Heyns, B. 78
Hirst, B. 16
Holmes, E. G. A. 12
Holt, J. 28, 30, 33, 34
Howe, M. J. A. 4, 26
Hughes, M. 22, 23–5, 69, 72
Hunter, R. 2
Hurt, J. S. 11

Illich, I. 40

Joffe, L. 13

Kanner, B. G. 14
Knowles, J. G. 3
Kulik, C.-L. C. 15
Kulik, J. A. 15

Lawrence, E. 10
Limbrick, E. 15
Lines, P. 2, 3, 112
Lloyd, P. 22
Locke, J. 10

McNaughton, S. 15
Marlow, S. 3
Mayberry, M. 3, 39
Meadows, S. 22
Meighan, R. 2, 3, 131
Middleton, D. J. 15
Montessori, M. 33

Neill, A. S. 28, 30

Palinscar, A. S. 15
Paterson, J. L. 3, 7, 28
Petrie, A. 2, 3
Pitman, M. A. 3, 6
Plowden Report 3, 12, 13

Quintilian 10